Faith Seeking

Faith Seeking

Denys Turner

scm press

British Library Cataloguing in Publication data

A catalogue record for this book is available
from the British Library

0 334 02888 4

First published in 2002 by SCM Press
9–17 St Albans Place, London N1 0NX

www.scm-canterburypress.co.uk

SCM Press is a division of
SCM-Canterbury Press Ltd

Typeset by Regent Typesetting
and printed in Great Britain by
Biddles Ltd, www.biddles.co.uk

Contents

The Intellectual Love of God

For Ruth, John and Brendan

'Heaven doth with us as we with torches do, not light them for themselves'

Measure for Measure, William Shakespeare, Act 1 Scene 1

Preface

That this collection of occasional lectures, talks and sermons turned out to possess any sort of thematic coherence at first surprised me when I found myself assembling them. Many academics would be apprehensive about making too much of the mass of varied papers which over time gathers on their shelves, representing talks given by invitation to this or that group, prepared, delivered and then forgotten about. And so I thought nothing much more of the pile thus accumulated than that my three children, Ruth, John and Brendan, might be interested some time to browse in it a little, if only out of curiosity. For these are pieces which have issued from the mind and experience of their academic father, though they have known more of the father, I suspect, than of his mind. And though most, but not all, were addressed to students and academics, only one, the first, was addressed to academics on an academic occasion. Many of them, therefore, *could have* been addressed to my children, indeed, one or two were.

In any case, I showed the collection, somewhat apprehensively, to a few good friends – among them Fr Christopher Hilton and Férdia Stone-Davis, who also compiled the index, research students in the Faculty of Divinity at Cambridge – who could be relied upon to be as honest as kind, and they seemed to think these pieces might deserve a wider readership. Kevin Loughton, Vittorio Montemaggi and Alexandra Wörn, likewise research students under my supervision at Cambridge, added helpful advice on some particular matters, and I am immensely grateful to all five of them for their help, but above all for the privilege of supervising their research. But even with their encouragement, I still would not have had the temerity to allow publication had not one of those friends also been that most excellent of theological publishers, Alex Wright of SCM Press, who offered to take responsibility for publishing them himself. I am also grateful to Philip Hillyer for some meticulous and sensitive copy-editing, and to Anna Hardman of SCM Press. I once had some responsibility for Anna when she was a PhD student in the Department of Theology at Birmingham. In her turn, she managed the considerably more demanding responsibility for me and my manuscript with efficiency, good judgment and courtesy. Above all, however, I owe debts of gratitude for the support and encouragement of Marie, my wife of thirty-three years.

I should explain a little of the thematic coherence which draws this collection together, for the pieces are of diverse kinds. Some are talks – delivered to businessmen, nurses, parishioners – some are lectures given to diverse audiences, but many are sermons, many of the latter, though not all, having been delivered in college chapels in my university. Such sermons are a curious *genre*, neither exactly parochial homily nor yet quite theological lecture, and they stand on the borderline which I have found myself so often crossing between the territory I occupy as an academic theologian, and the territory I occupy simply as a Christian, somewhere between the roles of teacher and of preacher. Of course, first and foremost, that borderline falls within my own mind and within my own life, and it is there that I have had to learn to cross it first. But after that – or perhaps in the course of seeking a way of crossing it personally – I have tried to do so in a public capacity, as discharging a duty of any Christian theologian, by means of the sort of 'cross-over' discourse which this collection represents. And though I have never thought of myself as a preacher in any common sense of that word (I should never have the presumption), I do think that there is a role for some members of the Church in offering a discourse to Christian minds which speaks of intellect in relation to, and as part of, Christian life. Indeed, if there is anything of which I have been trying to persuade the audiences and congregations I have spoken to outside the lecture hall, it is that intellect is a form of *life*, a necessary way of being *alive*, and that therefore doing theology is a way of being alive as a Christian, intrinsic to a Christian vocation.

I began my academic career as a philosopher, but in 1977 I moved from a Department of Philosophy in University College, Dublin to a Department of Theology and Religious Studies in the University of Bristol, and I have worked in such departments ever since, subsequently in Birmingham and now in Cambridge. I believed then, and believe now, that of all the academic disciplines in the university, theology was the one which could least afford, if it was equally prone to, any form of intellectual complacency. Of course, there is nothing so intellectually challenging in its nature that a university cannot be counted upon to tame it by some routine or other, or contain it – as the greater risk is today – by a pedagogical ideology and a managerialist apparatus of 'modularization' or of research- or teaching-quality 'assessment'. And even if I recognize – and *I* should know how to say this, I have been in my time an avowed Marxist – that religions of all kinds, not excluding Christianity, have a capacity to generate and sustain equally the most fanatically dangerous of other-worldly illusions and the most complacent of accommodations with a worldliness of spirit, nonetheless, I continue to find theology to be the means most apt to *unsettle*, to *rattle*, to *haunt* the mind with glimpses of something which, as Augustine thought, are very like long-lost memories, memories of the mystery of love from which we have come, sustaining a hope of the mystery of love we are destined for. For what good theology has the power to evoke is a sort of nostalgia for what all the rest of our education may have caused us to forget, a sense that what is *most* real is what escapes our grasp, resists containment *in* our minds even if that place of memory which it haunts is the best part *of* our minds. And good theology reminds us that that which our memory recalls us to has a name, the name of God. I would almost go so far as to say that it does not matter if students do not know that name so long as they experience that nostalgia, that longing, or as the Greeks called it, an *eros*, for our home, the place where we finally belong. For if once they come to know that longing, then they *can* get to know what the name 'God' names. Whereas if they have never experienced it, then they may call on the name as much as they like, but it will not name God, but only an idolatrous self-projection. After Spinoza I call that longing in one of the sermons which follows, the 'intellectual love of God'. And in that theme of loving God with the mind lies the coherency of this collection.

On the other hand, if in these talks and lectures and sermons I have tried to address intellects, and in doing so have tried to distil the best I have learned from the greatest minds of the Christian traditions, this has not been so as to fill them with those 'great' thoughts. I often advise students that they should not at any cost try to get Plato into their heads – which given the smallness of our minds by comparison with his would simultaneously diminish Plato and cause ache in our brains. Rather, they should try to get their heads into Plato. For there they will find a much vaster world of thought in which their minds can expand beyond all expectation. And I think in general this is the task of the Christian teacher and preacher: to invite minds out of the narrow regions of the already known – the 'real' world – into realities unknowable, realities so much larger and stranger than our mind's capacities that they can open up in the free air, into the wide, trackless oceans of the divine, and through expanded minds to acquire expanded hearts. It is for the teacher, therefore, but to *re*-mind, to restore to intellect this primordial *memory*, so as to make room for an infinite *love*, of which no one can be the cause or the occasion but that infinite love itself. Possessed by that love we know 'reality', for it is by love alone that we know that something other than ourselves is real. All that is not thus loved is 'known' but in the fantasies of an egoistic self-projection.

I cannot imagine what else a teacher, or for that matter a preacher, should do, except to *remind* people of their capacity for the infinite, and though I have no liking for the word 'spirituality', I should here venture to say that this teaching and learning is all by itself – needing nothing else to make it so – a 'spirituality', a way into the meaning of, and into the reality of, the Spirit, our only teacher. Jesus told us that we are not to call *ourselves* teachers, and God help us if, in our teaching and preaching, theologians should add anything of our own which does not contribute to that evincing of memory, that eliciting of nostalgia, that desire for the Spirit. All teachers know this humility, this diffidence, in practice, for they know that when they have taught well the students will spontaneously say: 'of *course*' – they *recognize*, as if recalling, a truth no longer the teacher's, because now commonly possessed and shared. Thus are we, teacher and student alike, restored to our home in the *real* real world.

None of the pieces in this collection was written with the others in mind, so although there is a certain thematic continuity and some overlap and repetition (which I have not sought to remove), they fell into no particular order other than that which I have loosely imposed by grouping them under broad section headings. Except that the first two longer and more technically difficult lectures (especially the first) in some sort lay the theological foundations for the rest, there is no good reason to read them in one order rather than another. All were written for oral delivery, none for publication, and so they were all spoken out loud to live audiences with eyes I was in a position to observe reactions in, and respond to. They should be read as such, in a manner as exchanges.

And speaking of eyes, the story is told of the Mullah Nasrudin, a Sufi mystic of the thirteenth century, who was once asked by a student how he had come to be so wise. 'That's easy', he replied. 'All day long I talk, morning, noon and night, I go on and on and on without ceasing. But as I talk, I look into people's eyes, and when I see a glint, I write down what I have just said.' What is to be found in this collection are those few remnants of some thirty- five years of my incessant talking which I noticed eliciting a glint. What hours of tedium betweentimes my long-suffering students have had to tolerate, what numbers of glazed eyes I have had to peer into from lectern and pulpit, in the meagre hope of that occasional glint, I do not care to calculate. At any rate readers are not thus captive, and unlike my students can take these words, or leave them, as they please.

Denys Turner
Peterhouse
University of Cambridge

The 'Otherness' of God

I

How to be an Atheist

The inaugural lecture is a difficult genre. New professors are encouraged to deliver them within a year or two of their appointment, though nowadays not all do, especially in the sciences. There is an element of ritual to them: in Cambridge, the University Vice-Chancellor likes to preside, perhaps to symbolize the fact that professors are appointed by and to the university, with a distinct responsibility to the university as a whole. That is bad enough for the new professor. To make matters worse, your colleagues in your Faculty like you to deliver an inaugural, because if they can count on you not to let them down, a good inaugural serves as a sort of 'shop-window', displaying to the wider university community the quality of the goods which we offer. And in a Faculty whose intellectual credentials have more often to be defended than those of most others, these can be important, and consequently nerve-racking, occasions. To add to these pressures there is one other, usually unspoken, factor: you know that all attending are expecting evidence that you were, after all, worthy to be appointed to your chair.

The problem for the new professor is how to do it: should you make appeal to those fundamental values of the intellectual life which all in the university share, and in terms which the heterogeneous audience which attends these occasions will understand – at the risk of generalizing blandness? Or should you speak to your specialist colleagues in terms others are unlikely to understand – at the risk of being merely precious? In this inaugural lecture, delivered in the Faculty of Divinity at Cambridge in October 2001, I tried to link these two purposes in the hope of avoiding either risk, and took a chance on not running both. In attempting to explain what is most fundamental to the theological enterprise – its peculiarly primitive questions – I wanted to show how theology is in fact an engagement, also of the most fundamental kind, with the purposes of a university, indeed, with the purposes of intellect itself. The mind is a form of life, a way of being alive; and the one sure way of ultimately refusing that life is by refusing to ask theological questions. That is 'how to be an atheist'.

When my colleague, Graham Stanton, the Lady Margaret's Professor, delivered his inaugural lecture some two years ago, he was able to do so in the presence of no less than two predecessors. I much regret that today I can bring forward none of mine in the Norris-Hulse Chair. For of such length was the tenure of my immediate predecessor, Professor Nicholas Lash, that none of his predecessors could reasonably have been expected to outlive his term of office, and he himself is perforce fulfilling obligations in Boston College. A pity, since I should have welcomed the opportunity to offer to him in person some tribute to the many qualities I have over the years admired in his work. An erudite scholar, he wears his learning lightly, preferring an energy and clarity of thought – 'wit' in an older meaning of the word – to mere quantity of annotation and reference; and since the virtue of clarity is to the life of the mind what humility is to the moral life – for as it indicates a willingness to be understood, so also it offers a vulnerability to refutation – there is that at least in which I should wish to emulate him.

Not that otherwise we have always agreed. Back in the early 1980s he and I published in quick succession monographs on the subject of Marxism and its relation to Christian theology. We agreed on much of a theological nature, disagreed sharply on how to read Marx, so Herbert McCabe, that most excellent of editors of *New Blackfriars* and a profound theological influence on us both, invited us each to review the work of the other, Nicholas first, me to follow. Herbert entitled my reply to Nicholas' review 'Turner Responds to Lash'. Well, today I mark my succession to Nicholas by means of a lecture which I am happy to concede is, in a manner, a response to the Lash's discipline, but in a spirit of emulation. For unfashionably – as theological fashion appears to have it today – I have decided to attempt an *intelligible* lecture, a lecture about a theological disagreement, but one clear enough, I hope, and containing a sufficient quantity of discernible and plain asseveration, that you will be able to disagree with it, if you think you should, or even conceivably to agree with it, if you think you can. For like Nicholas I follow Thomas Aquinas in thinking of theology, if indeed as rooted in a *sacra doctrina*, nonetheless as also *argumentativa*.

But because theology thrives on argument, I thought I would talk to you on the subject of how to be an atheist, at some risk of being thought patronizing – since I am not one myself. Of course I have an interest in there being an argument about the existence of God, for I have a subject to represent within the university and wider, and while no genuine interest would be served by picking a fight without intrinsic reason, subjects such as ours get some credit for their existence and cost when it is obvious to that community that they have an academic agenda of agreed significance, and that they engage in vigorous and settleable arguments over issues of general concern. Now, as to whether there is an argument to be had about the existence of God, opinion differs. There are those who wish to pick a fight with us over the question of whether there is or is not a God; but there are others who think that there is no fight worth picking, believing that the question doesn't matter because the answer, one way or the other, has consequences for no one but theologians. J. L. Austin, the Oxford philosopher of somewhat pedantic disposition, once rhetorically asked himself at the end of an especially trivializing paper on the subject of 'excuses', whether anyone could regard what he had claimed to demonstrate to be of any importance. To which he replied that importance was not important, only truth. Well, I think so too. All the same, importance is important to those who dispose of university funding, and my colleagues' jobs are at stake in the matter of having worthwhile issues to contest within the Divinity Faculty's division of academic labours. So, I have an interest of a vested sort in keeping the issue going of whether God exists, and of whether it matters to anyone else but us what the answer is.

As to those for whom the question does not matter, believing that nothing hangs on whether there is or is not a God, it is true that for very large sectors of the populations of Western countries, life is lived broadly in a mental and emotional condition of indifference to the question. And it is also true that, even among some intellectual elites, for many of whom it is fashionable to *allow* theism as an option within a generalized permissiveness of thought, the licence granted to theism can seem to amount to no more than a higher form of this more generalized and popular indifferentism. But such mentalities represent a different kind of challenge to the theologian than that posed by the orthodox and plain atheist and I shall come to the question of this 'higher indifferentism' later in this lecture. In the meantime, let us consider the matter of the good old-fashioned militant atheists, who flatter the theologian at least to the extent of seeing in the question of God a battleground of last resort, a final contest about the world, and about all that is in it, and about us.

Theologians, after all, are as easily seduced by the flattery of 'importance' as are any other academics, and there are some of our company who yearn for the good old days – perhaps they survived until the late nineteenth century – when it was still agreed that everything depended on whether or not there is a God, when it was still relatively clear what it was to think the existence of God, hence, what was to count as atheism was to the same extent unproblematical. In those good old days atheists knew what they were denying. For as Thomas Aquinas used to say, following Aristotle, *eadem est scientia oppositorum* – affirmations and their corresponding negations are one and the same knowledge – hence clarity about the affirmation permitted a clear-minded denial. In the mid nineteenth century, the German philosopher, Ludwig Feuerbach, was one such atheist: everything, he thought, that the theologian says about God is true; it is just that none of what the theologians say is a truth about *God*, all are truths about the human 'species-being', as he put it, and so in their theological form they are alienated truths. You have only to reverse subject and predicate, he says, turn God, the subject for theology, into the 'divine' as predicate of the human, and the alienated truths of theology become truths repossessed in humanism; thus, paradoxically, do you realize all the truth of theology in its abolition as atheism. Well, now, *there* is some flattery to the theologian, for in Feuerbach everything depends on the logically complete, and overtly theological, disjunction: either God or man, but not both. Indeed, so craven did he think Feuerbach's flattery of the theological to be that Karl Marx wished a plague to be visited on the disjunction itself, that is to say on the houses *both* of the theologian's God *and* on Feuerbach's humanist atheism, equally complicit did he think them to be in a theological view of the world. Feuerbach, Marx said, can no more get his humanism going without the negation of God than the theologian can get his theism going without the negation of man. Thus Marx. The twentieth-century Protestant theologian, Karl Barth, went even further than Marx in the exact specification of Feuerbach's theological parasiticalness, taking unseemly pleasure in the thought that, in the end, Feuerbach is his own atheist familiar, belonging, Barth says, 'as legitimately as anyone, to the profession of modern Protestant theology' (Karl Barth, 'An Introductory Essay' to Ludwig Feuerbach, *The Essence of Christianity*, trans. George Eliot, New York: Harper Torchbooks, 1957, p. xi): in truth, *eadem est scientia oppositorum*.

So it is possible to sympathize with those theologians who long for an energetic form of denial to grapple with, for it would reassure them in their hopes for a territory of contestation which has some sort of intellectual ultimacy about it: for note, our subject's interests are served not on condition that God exists, but on the less exacting condition that there is a decent argument to be had as to *whether* God exists. Alas, today, vigorous atheist opposition is hard to find, and I wish to help out; first, with the suggestion – just to clear some ground – that Marx might be right, that in much argument on the subject the complicity between theist and atheist, their common interest in the territory contested, is just too cosy, too mutually parasitical, too like the staged contest of a modern wrestling match. There might be some sort of entertainment in the antics, but there is no real edge to the competition.

And by way of illustrating this suspicion, let me risk a generalization from the particular form of opposition between Barthian theism and Feuerbachian atheism, whose character consists, as I think of it, as that between an object and its image in a mirror: all the connections of thought are identical, but their relations are, as it were, horizontally reversed from left to right. The generalization is that, historically, most philosophical, principled, not merely casual atheisms have in this way been mirror-images of a theism; that they are recognizable from one another, because atheisms fall roughly into the same categories as the theisms they deny; that they are about as interesting as one another; and that since narrowly Catholic or Methodist or Anglican atheisms are no more absorbing than narrowly Catholic, Methodist or Anglican theisms, neither offers much by way of a stimulus for the theologian.

And one reason for this atheistical failure of interest is its failure of theological radicalness: such atheists are but what are called 'negative' theologians, but attenuated ones. In a sense which I hope to clarify in a moment, they give shorter measure than good theologians do in the extent of what they deny. It is indeed extraordinary how theologically conservative some atheists are, and one might even speculate that atheists of this species have an interest in resisting such renewals of Christian faith and practice as would require the renewal of their rejection of it. I suppose it must be upsetting for atheists when the target of their rejection moves; for in so far as a moving Christian target does upset the atheist, it reveals, depressingly, the parasitical character of the rejection. So a static atheism can have no wish for a moving theism.

Of course the contrary proposition is equally plausible. There have always been Christian theisms which are parasitical upon forms of atheism, for they formulate a doctrine of God primarily in response to a certain kind of grounds for atheistic denial. In our time, the ill-named 'creationists' seem to offer a mere *reaction*, trapped as they are into having to deny the very possibility of an evolutionary world, simply because they mistakenly suppose an evolutionary world could be occupied only by atheists. Naturally, if you think you have to find a place for God somewhere in the universe, then you are going to have to expel a usurping occupant somewhere from it; and since our parasitical theist and atheist agree that evolutionary biology, or historical evidence, or cosmology, occupy the space where, were there a God, God ought to be, they are, as Nicholas used so often to point out, playing the *same* game, though alas for the theist, on rules of the atheist's devising. Hence, the theists play it on the undemanding condition that they play on the losing team.

It seems to me that that sort of argument between theist and atheist is entirely profitless to either side. But since today my purpose is to encourage the atheists to engage in some more cogent and comprehensive levels of denying, I shall limit my comment to saying that thus far they lag well behind even the *theologically* necessary levels of negation, which is why their atheisms are generally lacking in theological interest. So, I repeat: such atheists are, as it were, but theologians in an arrested condition of denial: in the sense in which atheists of this sort say God 'does not exist', the atheist has merely arrived at the theological starting-point. Theologians of the classical traditions, an Augustine, a Thomas Aquinas or a Meister Eckhart, simply agree about the disposing of idolatries, and then proceed with the proper business of doing theology.

And here is the sort of negative thing they then go on to do, at any rate in the medieval traditions in which I specialize. Thomas Aquinas tells us that he thinks he can give rational proofs of the existence of God, and gives us five ways of doing so. You will be pleased to hear that I have no intention of inflicting upon you any detail of those proofs, or even just now of discussing the matter of whether there could in principle be any such thing as a valid proof of the existence of God, though I will offer a few thoughts on the subject later. I ask you merely to note two things of a general sort about how Thomas Aquinas conceives of them. The first is that Thomas maintains that those proofs are not meant to tell you anything much about God at all, for rather they tell you something about the world, namely that it is *created*. Of course, what shows it to be created shows that we need to speak of its Creator. But, as I shall explain shortly, we could not properly know what it is that we are speaking of when we speak of God, for the creator of every manner and kind of thing cannot itself be a kind of thing, or an instance of anything. Hence, the two things we need to say about Thomas' 'proofs' of the existence of God are, first, that they are meant to show God to exist, and second, that they are meant to show we are bound to have lost most of our grip on the meaning of 'exists' as thus predicated of God.

And it is this second point which he explains immediately after he has presented his arguments for God's existence. He tells us that in any other discipline than theology, once you have shown that you have a subject-matter for it, the next thing you do is to ask about its nature and scope. In the previous discussion, then, he thinks that he has established the existence of something for theology to be about, namely God. So you might suppose, he says, that the next task is to give some account of what God is – as he puts it, you are likely to suppose that you need to establish the manner of God's existence, what sort of thing God is. But, alas for the vanity of theological ambitions, he insists on disappointing us. Here is how he puts it:

> Once you know whether something exists, it remains to consider how it exists, so that we may know of it what it is. But since we cannot know of God what he is, but [only] what he is not, we cannot inquire into the how of God ['s existence], but only into how he is not. So, the next thing to do is to consider this 'how God is not' . . . (*Summa Theologiae*, 1a, q3 Prol.)

Now I know that this will probably sound all rather too downbeat and unpromising of much for theology to do, since it appears to offer nothing in prospect for theology than the endless pursuit of a thought ever-vanishing into a trail of denials. But things could be worse, and for Thomas they are: the problem is not at all that theology has to battle against ordinary plain ignorance of what God is – as one might be ignorant of physics or biology – or by promethean effort of mind must seek to overcome the difficulties of knowing about a subject so distant from our ordinary experience. Rather, he says, the problem is the opposite: the real challenge for the theologian is not our ignorance of what God is, but rather that presented by those who think that they know what God is, for this is just idolatry. And that problem is presented to us equally by those theists who know all too well what they are affirming when they say 'God exists' and by those atheists – the mirror-image of the first – who know all too well what they are denying when they say 'God does not exist.' For both the affirmer and the denier are complicit in a sort of cosy and mutually reassuring idolatrous domesticity: in short, they keep each other in a job.

Thomas, however, will have none of this. Life is tougher both for the theist and for the atheist. God, Thomas says, is not any kind of thing. So you are but doing the theologian's day-job if you merely say, 'There is no such thing as God' – you might as well proclaim your atheist manifesto by denying Santa Claus (a matter I will come to a bit later). Thomas put it this way, in a sort of thought-experiment. Suppose you were to count up all the things in the world on some lunatic project of counting, all the things that there are, have been and will be, and suppose they come to the number n. Then I say, 'Hold on, I am a theist and there is one being you haven't yet counted, and that is the being who created them all, God'; would I be right to say that now the sum total of things is n+1? Emphatically no. God could not be both the creator of all things visible and invisible and one of things created, an additional something, not even a *unique* additional something: for there cannot be a kind of thing such that logically there can only be one of them. Of course, the final autograph of Beethoven's C sharp minor quartet is unique, there cannot be more than one of them, but that is simply a tautology, for its being described as 'final' attaches a uniqueness designator to it, and does not describe it as a 'kind'; but it is still countable as one in the series of Beethoven's final autographs. Whereas, as Thomas says, although the word 'God' is not the proper name of an individual, but a word we *use* in the way in which we use descriptions, still we have no proper *concept* which answers to it. Having no proper concept of God, we possess no account of the kind of thing God is; hence, we have no way of identifying God as an *instance* of any kind. After all, this follows because of what, if indeed you have proved God to exist, you have proved the existence of. What shows God to exist equally shows God's unknowability. And of course I do not expect you to believe all that: after all, I am here trying to encourage the atheists, not the theists, to have a decent go at denying God. All I am saying to the atheists is that they had better sharpen up a bit on their denials, for on the score so far, Thomas is well ahead.

That said, now for some words of encouragement for the atheists, for, poor bewildered things, having abandoned a merely parasitical anti-fundamentalism, they must by now be feeling quite at a loss to know how to set about denying God. First, though, a warning about some unhelpful advice which you might get from your philosophical friends if the point has not already occurred to you for yourselves. You might be tempted at this stage impatiently to protest: 'If you, the theists, won't affirm anything at all, and in effect you have not, then why do we, the atheists, need to do any denying, because you theologians have already done all the denying there is to be done? Does not your so-called "negative theology" amount to little more than a strategy of evasion which kills God off by a death of a thousand qualifications? You say "God exists", but you add: "in no knowable sense"; is "one", but you qualify: "not as countable in a series"; is "good", but not, you say, "on any scale", not even on the top of one. Might not your negative theologians just as well be atheists as affirm so incomprehensible a God? Only give us something affirmed and we will at last have something to deny. All you are doing is endlessly postponing God: so all we have to do is tag along while you get on with the denials we thought it was our job to deal in and wait until you actually affirm something, which, by the sound of your Thomas Aquinas, you are never going to get round to doing.'

Now as an atheist response to theologians, this line of attack, though promising, is not yet quite fair. There *is* something which theists affirm, namely that the world is created. That, they think, is our starting-point for talking about God, and so long as we remain resolutely anchored in the implication of that starting-point – that theologians are *always* speaking of the ultimately ungraspable, that we do not know what God is – the theologians can feel justified in all manner of talk about God, and can safely and consistently allow that everything true of creation, everything about being human, is in some sort grounds for a truth about God. Negative theology does not mean that we are short of things to say about God; it means just that everything we say of God falls short of him.

The theologians, therefore, howsoever 'negative' of disposition, need not be quite so slippery creatures as would reduce their position to a form of theological postmodernism, a position of endless *deferral*, according to which there is only postponement, only *pen*ultimacy, an endlessly contingent 'otherness', no rest in any ultimate signifier which could stabilize the whole business of signification upon a foundational rock of fixed and determinate reference. But at what price do the theologians at the last minute draw back from so extreme a negativity? Might not the theologians now be differently accused – precisely because they do not want to go so far down the postmodern road of an intellectual nihilism – of a form of intellectual cheating, of attempting to eat their cakes and have them? On the one hand, they will say, with the emphatic negativity of – to quote another negative theologian – a Meister Eckhart: God is a 'being transcending being and a transcending nothingness' (*Sermon 83, Renovamini Spiritu*, in Edmund Colledge and Bernard McGinn (eds.), *Meister Eckhart: The Essential Sermons, Commentaries, Treatise and Defense*, New York, NY: Paulist Press, 1981, p. 207); on the other, they will take back with unblushing affirmativeness what they have just apophatically given away, and add a good, plain, unproblematical, undeconstructed existential '*there is*' one such. And are not the hidden theological interests betrayed at the last minute by that surreptitious '*there is*', howsoever negative-sounding and 'apophatic' you get the description to be which follows it? Would not the theologians be *obliged* thus to cheat if they are to make any claim to a theism which does not simply collapse into the nihilism of a Derrida or of a Nietzsche, who famously thought that getting rid of God required the abandonment of all grammar? But the theologians cannot have it both ways: either, in a sort of reversal of Nietzsche, they can have his grammar, and his 'there is a . . .' is a plain, ordinary existential assertion in good grammatical form, in which case it cancels the apophaticism of the description asserted to exist, and God is just another, ordinary 'thing-in-the-world'; or else the existential claim is cancelled as affirmative utterance by the apophaticism, in which case you have no ordinary, defensible, sense of '. . . exists' affirmed. Are we not then simply back to square one, forced to choose between an idolatrous affirmation and a negativity indistinguishable from atheism, with no third possibility falling between them?

I think at this point things are looking up for the atheists, though they are still not quite all the way to determining how to contest with a negation on terms adequate to the theologians' affirmation. For though it is true, as I said, that the theologians do affirm something the atheists can deny, we need to look a little more carefully at what it is that the theologians affirm, and it may not be quite what the atheists were expecting. The minimum the theologian cannot deny is that the world is created. 'Out of nothing'. And you get to say that by entertaining a question which the assertion 'God exists' answers to. It is a question about the world. It is a logically odd question about the world, but still a question with an intelligible sense: it is the question with which, in one or other version, each of Thomas' five ways ends: 'Why is there anything at all, rather than nothing at all?' for it is the legitimacy of the *question* which those arguments purport to demonstrate, that is to say that it has to have an answer. It is not their purpose to place in our hands some knowable answer to it. It is an intelligible question, because it stands at the top end of a scale of questions which are all unproblematically intelligible and is intelligibly connected with them. For you can ask of anything whatever in the world, 'Why does it exist, rather than something else?' and you ask it, in the relevant sense, in one of the many disciplines of enquiry in which we human beings engage, most of which we call 'science'. And I do not see why, if that is so, you cannot ask not alone of this or that, or of this or that kind of thing, why it exists, but why anything at all should exist rather than nothing.

You might disagree; you might think the question does not make sense, as Bertrand Russell did on a famous occasion in discussion with Frederick Copleston on the BBC radio Third Programme, when he said that all you can say about the world, however it has come about, is that it is 'just there, that's all'. There can't be a question: 'How come there is *anything* there?' because you could not give any account of the answer, the business of accounting for things belonging within the world; it can have no purchase on anything which might count as the cause of it. Now that is something we can argue about as theist does with atheist. For my part, I think it is an intelligible question, one the answer to which would bear the name 'God'. And I cannot see why you should want to prevent me asking it.

On the other hand, one has to admit, like Russell, that it is a logically odd question, and just how odd can be best understood from its eccentric syntax. Attend to the 'rather than'. We can get this relational expression going when we can supply symmetrical values for the variables 'p' and 'q' in the expression 'p rather than q': for

example, 'red rather than green'. The 'rather than' has the force of
an intelligible contrast because red and green are both colours, and
so we know what they differ *as*. But what are you to make of the 'p
rather than q' if I substitute 'red' for p and 'Thursday' for q? – for it
would seem odd to consider what 'red' and 'Thursday' differ *as*. All
the same, as Chomsky says, no nonsense phrase is beyond all possible reach of some context which could make sense of it, and since I
happen to think of days of the week as having colours, in that
context it makes perfectly good sense to contemplate the disjunction
'red rather than Thursday', though admittedly it is the rather special
one in which Thursdays are blue. But while you are thinking about
the eccentric thing you have got 'rather than' up to in this case, let
me add to your burdens: What oddity have you inflicted upon
'rather than' if you substitute 'anything whatever' as a value for p
and 'nothing' as a value for q? Has the '. . . rather than . . .' any
meaning left – is it still intelligible? In a way, yes, it is intelligible; it
has the force of a very radical sort of 'might have been . . .'.

A thing which is red, like a letter box in the UK, might have been
green, as letter boxes are in Ireland, but there are no doubt good
reasons why they are red in the UK and green in Ireland, some prior
states of affairs which account for the colours they are – providing a
causal narrative, you might say. But if we could imagine that rather
than there being anything at all there might have been nothing at all,
we have, indeed, some force of contrast going for our '. . . might
have been . . .' but not one you could give any account of in terms of
antecedent states of affairs, no possible Chomskyan context to make
sense of it, no explanatory causal narrative, for *a fortiori* there is
nothing left to account for the fact that there is something rather
than nothing, no bit of the world there functioning to explain the
existence of things, but only nothing. And 'nothing', as Thomas says,
is not a peculiar sort of causally explanatory something, it is not an
antecedent condition; nor, alternatively, is there some specialized
theological sense which might give force to that sort of 'out of'
which is 'out of nothing'. The expression 'out of nothing' means, he
says, just the contrary, for the negation negates the 'out of . . .' itself,
as if to say: 'not out of anything' – we have a making here, but no
'out of', no antecedent conditions, so no process, no event; an after,
but no before.

Therefore, when you ask of the world, 'How come that anything
at all exists?' you are not asking an as yet unsolved question of

empirical fact, because you are not asking *any* sort of empirical question: as Wittgenstein demonstrates in the *Tractatus*, there is no possible sense of 'fact' in which 'that there is anything at all' can be a fact, Russellian 'brute' or otherwise. When you ask that question you are merely giving expression to something you know about the world: it is a state of affairs which might not have been, that's the sort of world we have: that it exists at all has been *brought about*.

Now an empiricist, upon hearing that the statement '*that* there is anything at all has been brought about' is not a 'factual' statement, will quite naturally conclude that it is not a proper proposition at all, but just the expression of a sort of non-propositional *attitude* towards the world, the sort you could choose to adopt or not without offence to facts or evidence either way. But it is clear that Thomas Aquinas drew no such conclusion, for he thought it *demonstrable* that the world is created, and non-propositional attitudes cannot be demonstrated. And of course it is just here that he is in trouble not just with the atheist but also with the most common sort of theist of our own times. Notoriously he is in trouble with Kant, who thought that you could get causal questions and answers going within the world, but that in principle you could not make sense of a causal explanation of the fact that there is one at all. But for me, a much more enjoyable part of daily academic life than being out of sorts with Kant, is the fact that I find myself in constant debate with most of my friends here – colleagues in the Faculty and graduate students in our 'God' seminar – who disagree with me on much of this, though not all of it. I think most of us agree that the statement 'the world is created' is a proposition capable of being true or false, and further that it is a true proposition. But they are endlessly telling me that I am wrong both in claiming that a purely rational causal proof of God is possible and in thinking that Thomas offers one.

On the score of the first, more general, disagreement, sometimes the appeal against proof is made on epistemological grounds of the sort found in Kant's *Critique of Pure Reason*, sometimes on the theological ground, also found there, that you must deny reason its demonstrations in order to leave room for faith; but more recently another, now former, Cambridge theologian, John Milbank has appealed to an argument of formal logic in Aristotle's *Posterior Analytics*. He tells me that a supposititious causal proof of the existence of God is bound to be formally invalid by the fallacy of equivocation, since the sense of 'cause' in the premises could not be the same as the sense of 'cause' in the conclusion supposedly entailed. Now Aristotle maintains that any deductive inference constructed from premises whose terms belong to one genus, to a conclusion whose terms belong to another genus, must fail by equivocation, for, as he puts it, scientific explanation and inference cannot thus 'skip' generic gaps. But if Aristotle forbids inferences which 'skip' the finite distance between one *genus* and another, how much the more, Milbank insists, must an inference be prohibited which purports to skip the *infinitely bigger* gap between any *genus* and a being which transcends *all possible genera*. In either case, the inference would fail by the fallacy of equivocation; and if in the theological case it did not fail for that reason, this could be only because it fails for the opposite reason. For if the sense of 'cause *of* the universe' were the same sense as that of 'cause *in* the universe' – if 'cause' were predicated univocally in premises and conclusion – then you would get a valid inference all right, but to an idolatrously worldly conception of God as just another, worldly, cause. Hence, a causal proof is either formally invalid because equivocal, or else valid because relying on an idolatrous univocity.

To which argument (by the way, it owes everything to Duns Scotus and nothing to Thomas Aquinas) of necessity all too briefly, I reply: validity is as validity does – or as the scholastics used to say, *ab esse ad posse valet illatio*. There cannot be a *general* case against arguments from premises to conclusions not univocally continuous with them, for we can easily construct counter-instances. Geach quotes one from Quine: from the relational term, '. . . smaller than . . .' and the general term, 'visible', both belonging to the universe of things which we can directly observe, we can form the compound term, 'smaller than any visible thing', which is in perfectly sound logical order, yet could not, *a fortiori*, have application within that same universe of directly observable objects. As Quine points out: the compound gets us out of the universe within which the uncompounded terms both have application, 'without a sense of having fallen into gibberish'. He adds, 'The mechanism is of course analogy, and more specifically extrapolation' (W. V. O. Quine, *Word and Object*, Cambridge, Mass.: MIT Press, 1960, p. 109, and Peter Geach, 'Causality and Creation' in *God and the Soul*, London: Routledge & Kegan Paul, 1969, pp. 80–1). Now what holds for this simple compounding will hold for any argument whose premises contain the simple uncompounded terms and the conclusion the terms thus compounded: what holds is that such an argument will not fail of the fallacy of equivocation. On the other hand, those premises will, on condition of the formal validity of the argument, entail a conclusion whose terms are not univocally related to the premises. Now what holds for Quine's case, holds equally for one of Geach's on the score of inferential validity: an argument, if it could be constructed, whose premises contained the uncompounded terms, '. . . cause of . . .' and 'every mutable thing', both having univocal application within the domain of our human, natural, rational experience, would not fail of the fallacy of equivocation just because the conclusion entailed was the existence of the 'cause of every mutable thing'. On the other hand, since it would be clear that the relational term '. . . cause of . . .' in the conclusion could not be understood in the same sense as it is understood in the premises, the argument would trade in no theologically offensive univocity, thereby reducing God to 'just another cause'. For the argument would have demonstrated the necessity of an analogical extrapolation which could not have been presupposed to it.

But you may be caused to protest – as one PhD student did the other day, causing me hurriedly to write this next bit – that the two cases are crucially different: for is not God *infinitely* different from any creature? What may hold for inferences from one *genus* of creatures to another – even if Quine is right – cannot be supposed to hold between any creatures and God, for the 'othernesses' in question are not comparable, the one being finite, the other infinite, and in the latter case the gap to be crossed by inference must be unbridgeable, no rational argument could possibly get you across it. Well, *you* might not be caused thus to protest, but John Milbank was, in an email sent from the depths of Virginia when I put Geach to him, and though I should not think it fair to take him on here without right of reply, I think I may fairly make one comment of a kind with which I know he anyway agrees.

You say: 'God's difference from creatures is incomparable with any creaturely difference.' Just so. But God's difference is not 'incomparably *greater*', as if to say: it is of this kind or that, only *infinitely* so. You cannot say, 'the difference between chalk and cheese is of *this* kind, and the difference between God and cheese is of *that* kind – see how incomparably different the two differences are!' We philosophers in the Divinity Faculty all get on famously with each other agreeing that God 'is not any kind of being'; but, that being so, it follows that we should not fall out over *how* God is different from every created being which *is* of some kind, belonging, as one says, to some *genus* or other; for if God is not any kind of being, then his difference from creatures is not a *difference* of any kind, hence, is not incomparably greater, but, on the contrary, is, simply, *incommensurable*. So, if we have a problem about inferences across different sizes of gap between creatures, we should be cautious of too readily supposing that, in the matter of God, 'size of gap' can in any way come in to it. That, as Nicholas Lash puts it, is just to make a mistake of theological grammar.

I apologize that all this is excessively condensed and, in the absence of a fuller explanation of these obscure thoughts, can I try a more theological tack? I sympathize with any Christian theologians who think that, in their proper concern to defend the divine 'transcendence', they should go in for maximizing gaps between God and creatures to an infinite degree of difference; but I think it not helpful to put it this way, and that if they insist on doing so, they should consider how, consistently with such a strategy, they will approve of Augustine's fine words: 'But you, O Lord, were more *intimate* to me than I am to myself' – *tu autem eras interior intimo meo* (*Confessions*, 3.6.7); for Augustine's sense of the divine 'otherness' is such as to place it, in point of transcendence, *closer* to my creaturehood than it is possible for any creatures to be to each other: for creatures are more distinct from each other than God can possibly be from any of them. The logic of transcendence is not best embodied in metaphors of 'gaps', even infinite ones, and if we must speak in such metaphors, we should at least acknowledge that, since we are in possession of no account of the gap to be crossed between God and creatures, it is difficult to see what force there is to the objection that rational inference could not cross it.

Now if you will permit me that much – and to be quite honest you should not do so without a lot more argument – then we have some support for the legitimacy of the question: 'Why is there something rather than nothing?' and we know that whatever the answer is we are led to contemplate a cause beyond our ordinary understanding of causes. And if we say, as Thomas does, that whatever the answer is, it is 'what people refer to when they talk of "God"', then we know at least one thing about God: we know that we could not know what it means to say 'God exists' because the notion of existence has now run off the edge of our intelligible world, even if it was necessities of thought about our world which led us to it: before God, language has, as it were, run *itself* out of the possibilities available to it. So we have to conclude that to assert 'God exists' is to make an existential claim in a perfectly ordinary sense of 'exists' because there is no other available to us, there being no special theological or religious sense of 'existence' available to do for the existence of God. But that being so, and for no other reason, I know that what requires me to say 'God exists' is true also denies me a grasp on what it means to say it. Therefore, if you, dear atheist, are to deny what I affirm, I must insist that you know how to deny all that follows from what I affirm. And it follows from what I affirm that, if there is an answer to that question, then we could not possibly know what it is: it could not be any kind of thing. So to repeat: it is no use supposing that you disagree with me if you say, 'There is no such thing as God'. For I got there well before you. What I say is merely: the world is created out of nothing, *that's* how to understand God. Deny that, and you are indeed some sort of decent atheist. But note what the issue is between us: it is about the legitimacy of a certain very odd kind of intellectual curiosity, about the right to ask a certain kind of question.

Let me therefore conclude with a few lightweight remarks about that business of asking very odd questions – the sort that you can make sense of asking, but not a lot of the answer. They are, if you like, rather infantile questions: adult questions are questions you have some sort of control over, questions you have disciplined procedures for dealing with, since the sense of the questions determines what kind of answers stand as good answers to them. This symmetry between questions and answers is simply what we mean by scientific method. Scientific questions are adult, intelligible questions demanding sensible answers arrived at by explicitly controlled methodologies. Theological questions, on the other hand, are childish: and this thought came to mind a while ago when I read in a newspaper report that Richard Dawkins had said that belief in the existence of God is childish, like belief in Santa Claus or in the Tooth Fairy.

Now I am not very sure what Dawkins does understand, but he clearly does not understand children if he thinks that the childishness of theism makes theism like belief in Santa Claus and the Tooth Fairy. For Santa Claus and the Tooth Fairy are adult stories and children do not spontaneously believe in them. Children only believe in Santa Claus and the Tooth Fairy because adults persuade them to, and often for unimpressive reasons of their own, like contriving cover for the choice of inappropriate presents; whereas theism is closely connected not with adult myths foisted upon children, but with more spontaneous forms of thought which are natural to children's own minds; and adults seem often to want to suppress such childish thoughts, seeing that they energetically set about systematically destroying a child's capacity for them by means, principally, of compulsory education in properly ordered questions which you can answer in accordance with teachable methodological routines. This is nowadays called the 'core curriculum', or otherwise what you are being asked to do when you spell out your 'aims and objectives'.

Now you may have observed how children seem quite early to rumble this adult conspiracy to educate them into asking only sensible questions, for they soon learn the joys of irritating adults with truly offbeat questions; and when it comes to theology, Thomas is a pure child. For the child asks the question 'Why?' once too often, where 'once too often' means: when there is no intellectual possibility of understanding an answer, where science and knowledge run out of things to say, indeed where reality itself has run out of things which can be said about it – in other words where language itself has run out. And that, for Thomas, is where theology begins, with a question so childish that now it is adult answers which are irrelevant and an impertinence: 'Why is there something rather than nothing?' That is a question to which it is essential that premature and merely adult answers be ruled out, for the question could not have the sort of answer which you would expect from good science. Philosophers seem happy enough to say, after Aristotle, that philosophy begins in wonder. Alas, all too often their philosophy ends in its elimination. Instead of leaving us, as it were, in a condition of *instructed* awe – what Nicholas of Cusa called a *docta ignorantia* – it leaves us instead with Russell's blank and indifferent stare: that there is anything at all is just a brute fact.

On the other hand, as I have argued, too often theologians I think of as parasitical want to jolly things up with a quite mistaken and idolatrous account of how theology makes a difference, hoping to find for themselves a purchase on something to say that others cannot, a *particular* difference that their theism makes to our ordinary routine ways of explaining things. They will derive little comfort in such hopes from Thomas Aquinas. For him, to say that the world is created adds nothing at all to our information about the kind of world we have got. As Thomas, who thought the world is created, said in reply to Aristotle, who thought that it is not, the difference between a created and an uncreated world is no difference at all so far as concerns how you describe it; any more, as later Kant said, the difference between an existent and a non-existent dollar can make a difference to what a dollar is. For Thomas, the logic of '. . . is created' is the same as the logic of '. . . exists': an uncreated X and a created X cannot differ in respect of what an X is, and so to say that the world is created makes not the least difference to how you do your science, or your history, or read your literatures; it does not make that kind of *particular* difference to anything. The only difference it makes is *all* the difference to everything.

And what kind of difference is that? Just this. What you mark by way of difference in saying that the world is created out of nothing is that it stands before us not in some brute, unmeaningful Russellian 'just thereness', in that sense as something just 'given' in which further questions are gratuitously ruled out, and that just at the point where they are beginning to get really interesting. Rather, in saying that the world is created out of nothing, you are beginning to say that the world comes to us, our existence comes to us, from an unknowable 'other'; that is to say, you are claiming that existence comes to us as pure gift, that for the world to exist just *is for it to be created*. As for why it exists, goodness only knows what the reason is. Of course, it might be the case that the world exists for a reason which *only* an omnipotent goodness knows, as a sort of act of love. But that would be another story which we could not tell for ourselves, but only if we were told it first, as a sort of *second*, super-added, gift.

In the meantime, what is at stake between the theist and the atheist? What is at stake is an issue which is, after all, central to our preoccupations as academics here, to our university responsibilities as such. It is an issue about the nature of *intellect*, and about how to take responsibility for all that it is capable of, about how to respond to the demands which, of its nature, it makes on us to persist. It is about the legitimacy of a certain kind of question and about whether it can be right to set *a priori* limits to a capacity which is, as Aristotle says, potentially infinite; which being so, Thomas Aquinas adds, it is not going to be satisfied – that is to say, enjoy any question-stopping complacency in – even an *infinite* object. Deny that, and you do, for certain, deny God and you have got your atheism in one move. But in denying the legitimacy of the question you also deny intellect its nature, which, as I have argued, you can just as easily do with bad theology, for *eadem est scientia oppositorum*.

So, 'How to be an atheist'? It is not easy; you need to work at it. Be intellectually adult, get an education, get yourself a discipline; resist all temptation to ask such questions as you do not know in principle can be answered, being careful to suppress any which might seem to push thought off civilized limits; be reasonable, lest you find yourself being committed to an excessive rationality; and have the good manners to scratch no itches which occur in intellectually embarrassing places – at least in public. Then I shall argue with you on behalf of the child, not in the name of God but in the name of a question which remains about the world, not yet in the name of theology, but in the name, merely, of an intellectual possibility you have excluded, not on account of *how* the world is, which seems a relatively sensible and obvious state of affairs to me, but out of amazement of intellect, and a sort of primal gratitude of spirit, that there is anything at all, rather than nothing, and that there is any*one* at all, rather than no one, for whom it exists. For, of the two possibilities there are, that there is anything at all must be by far the more unlikely outcome. If you want to be an atheist, then, it is necessary only to find *that the world is* to be a platitudinously dull fact. But, I warn you, to be as resolute as it takes in the conviction of such cosmic dullness requires much hard work, not a little training, and a powerful mental asceticism. Anything less resolute, and you run the risk of affliction by theological itches which, the atheists will no doubt be distressed to hear, my theological colleagues and I will be paid at the same rate as them to scratch.

2

How to be a Heretic

This talk continues some of the themes of the last. It was delivered in September 2000 to a general audience in Wells Cathedral at the invitation of its Chancellor, the Revd Melvyn Matthews, an old friend whom I had first known when he was Anglican Chaplain at the University of Bristol and I was a lecturer in the Department of Theology and Religious Studies. It was the last in a series on 'Radical Orthodoxy' and rather than directly address the issues raised by the earlier speakers, who were all in one way or another associated with that broad movement of theological and ecclesial reform which originated in Cambridge in the late 1990s, I chose to highlight the contemporary predicament of the heretic, just as in the previous lecture I had tried to highlight the contemporary predicament of the atheist. It is hard-going being a heretic when everything is permitted, including orthodoxy, and an ill-defined 'postmodernism', reread as an ideology of relativism, is the most reactionary stance of all, since it robs even heresy of its radicalness. In this, and rather more simply in the next two pieces, I try to explain how a Christian mentality is but a hair's breadth apart from a broadly 'postmodern'; also, why that hair's breadth of a difference is all the difference in the world, all the difference there ever is between heresy and orthodoxy.

G. K. Chesterton once said that whereas in former times – I think he meant in the Middle Ages – everyone, even the most heretical, thought of themselves as orthodox, today – and of course here he had in mind the early years of the twentieth century – the claim to be a heretic is a matter of self-congratulation, the heretic expects applause for his interesting unorthodoxy. As usual, Chesterton's paradox contains an illuminating grain of truth. It was true, in the Middle Ages, that heretics would endure the vilest tortures rather than admit to heresy, for them it was their torturers who had departed from some central truths of the orthodox tradition. Even the so called 'Free Spirit' heretics of the thirteenth and fourteenth centuries denied that they were, in any modern sense, 'free thinkers': they saw themselves as the radicals because they were holding on to the mainstream, the tradition, the primitive core of truth which that tradition contained, from which their tormentors had, they thought, departed. And I think it was probably true also, in Chesterton's time, that the contrary thought prevailed: the best minds of his age often found pride and dignity in the proclamation of their heretical opinions: indeed they had hardly anything else to take pride in except in the character of their opinions as heretical.

But – offering one generalization in exchange for another with about the same degree of truth – in our times things seem different yet again: today, it is hardly possible to be a heretic at all, and this is because it seems no longer possible to be orthodox. For, as you will know, heresy is a parasite, it feeds off the body-orthodox – as Socrates put it, it is like a gad-fly goading the slumbering horse of orthodoxy into conscious life. Now the metaphor of a body-orthodox is worth attending to. An orthodoxy is not just a collection of truths: it is truths whose authenticity is guaranteed and policed by an authoritative community which in some privileged way claims the status of their bearer, claims to embody them, claims the right to proclaim them and to determine the boundaries which separate those truths from error. The medieval heretic acknowledged that: he, or sometimes she, merely noted that, for this reason or that, the Church which made claims to be the body-orthodox had lost the right to do so. The medieval heretic was a reformer of the Church in the name of orthodoxy; but today, there is no possibility of heresy because we have denied the possibility of Church; not merely that the Church actually possesses the truth therefore, for we have denied also the very possibility of a community which is the authoritative bearer of it.

Let me tell you a medieval story. On 1 June 1310, a woman known as Marguerite Porete was burned at the stake in the Place de Grèves in Paris for having continued to circulate, after its prohibition by her bishop, the manuscript of her book, *A Mirror of Simple Souls*. Historians and theologians can find layer upon layer of significance in the details of the story, of her person, of her text. She was a woman, a fact which alone threatened a certain male theological hegemony; she wrote in Old French, by which her thoughts were made accessible to a much wider audience than the latinate theological authorities could imagine prudent; she had no formal theological training, no qualifications on which to rest the authority of her message, but only that of her own words and experience; but worst of all, without any of these means of professional access to the theological traditions, this amateur showed a subtlety of knowledge of those traditions – she knew them well enough to parody the conventional theological formulae of the Schools – and that, of course, then, as now, was calculated to enrage the professionals.

Yet for all that, it is wrong to cast her in the role of a mystical dissident. She thought of herself as orthodox. She managed to elicit the endorsement for her theology from three male expert theologians, one of them, Godfrey of Fontaines, a prestigious Master of Theology at the University of Paris who, though admitting that her opinions were capable of misrepresentation, deemed them fundamentally sound and orthodox. And then there is the startling fact that, after her execution, her text disappeared from circulation for some thirty years or so, only to re-emerge, in widespread distribution throughout Europe, no longer attributed to the heretic Marguerite and, being thought to have been written by a man, was judged to present no serious theological challenge. Indeed, as late as 1926, the Cardinal Archbishop of Westminster granted an *imprimatur* to a modernized English version of *The Mirror*, an edition which still ascribed authorship to 'an unknown male of the fourteenth century'.

All these facts provide us with a sort of test-case of the meaning of heresy and orthodoxy. But what tells us most about that meaning is what she says in that brilliantly insightful, but ill-organized and rambling, text. She speaks of the 'annihilated soul', the soul who has become nothing but the presence of God, a soul which has become entirely free because moved by no desires of its own, not even, she says, by the desire to conform to the will of God. This is because her will has *become* the divine will, her love is one with and indistinguishable from the divine love, she loves God with that absolute divine freedom which lives, and loves, and wills, as she puts it in one of her most characteristic phrases, 'without a why'; for she loves God by means not of her own love, but by means of that love which is God. There are such liberated souls, she says, and they, collectively, constitute what she calls 'Holy Church the Great', lying hidden, unobserved, forgotten within the bosom of 'Holy Church the Less'. Holy Church the Less, on the other hand, is the Church of those who are not yet free, of those whose actions are dictated by their finitely good desires, who love God with reasons and purposes and ends of their own, who live under the obligations of the moral law, who will what is virtuous because constrained by the demands and obligations of virtuous living, constrained by their dependence on the sacramental and devotional economies of the Church. They are good, Christian souls; Holy Church the Less is not the 'less' because it is corrupt, but because unliberated souls seek the good without freedom of spirit and for reasons of their own, out of their own wills: and they are therefore unliberated because the good which they seek is the finite good which a finite human capacity can make its own. They live therefore not as those free souls live who will out of the infinite capacity of the divine love itself, for they are captive within the limits of their own wills.

Now it is not really surprising that Marguerite's inquisitors believed her to be offering a pure antinomianism, the doctrine that those who have achieved some higher spiritual condition live beyond the constraints of ordinary morality and the pedestrian constraints of good Christian living. All the more might they have felt entitled so to judge her work when they read the dialogue which she constructs between Love, who represents her Holy Church the Great, the soul, which is herself, and Reason, representing Holy Church the Less. Here is how part of it goes:

Love: Once a soul has reached this state [of annihilation], she can say to the virtues: 'I have no further need of you, now I have served you all this time'.

The Soul: I agree, dear Love. I was their servant, but your kind courtesy has set me free from enslavement to them. Virtues, I leave you behind forever! My heart is now freer and more at peace than it has ever been. It was hard work being your servant, that I know well. For a time I put my heart inseparably into your service and you knew it: I was completely given over to you, therefore then I was your slave, but now I am released, and I wonder how I was able to escape.

Love: This soul knows no care, has neither shame nor honour, neither poverty nor riches, neither joy nor sorrow, neither love nor hate, neither hell nor heaven.

Reason: For God's sake, Love, what are you saying?

Love: What I mean can only be understood by those to whom God has given understanding and by none other; it is not taught by Scripture, nor can human reason work it out . . . It is a gift received from the Most High, in whom all knowing leads to loss of understanding . . . So this soul that has become nothing possesses all and possesses nothing, knows all and knows nothing, wills everything and wills nothing.

Reason: Lady Love, how can this be, you said before that this soul has no will? How, then, can she will everything and will nothing?

Love: Because, dear Reason, it is not the soul's will that wills, but God's will willing in her; the soul does not rest in love as if led to it by any desires of her own. Rather, love rests in her, takes over her will, and has her will of her. So now love can work in the soul without the soul's will, and the soul will be freed from all cares.

Now it is very important to read this passage with attention. Marguerite does not tell us that the liberated soul can act in spite of the virtues, is free of the virtues in the sense that she can with spiritual justification act contrary to what virtue commands. She says something much more radical than that – and I mean that she seems to understand that there is nothing more conventionally parasitical, little so ultimately conformist, as that protest against morality which consists simply in acting immorally. Breaking the rules gets its meaning from the rules it breaks; adultery pays its homage to marital fidelity, the burglar shows respect for the law of property without which his burglary lacks possibility: these rule-breaking stratagems do futile honour to the moral law they infringe as in its ultimate form the futility of Satan's defiance in *Paradise Lost* is consummated in a desperate admission of its defeat: 'evil, be thou my good'.

Not such is Marguerite's defiance. The annihilated soul, she says, does all that virtue requires, but not as required; she does all that the Church commands, but not as commanded. She does as one free of obligation exactly that which the unfree soul does as the slave of it. For the liberated soul needs nothing, acts out of no obligation to anything given, precedent to her act: in her words, the soul which is nothing acts and wills out of her nothingness. So this soul, she says, does all that the Church commands, but does not need the Church to command it. Now this is true heresy: not, that is, to dissent from orthodoxy, not to depart from orthopraxis, for that is easy and has no character of the radical about it. The true heresy lies in not needing to need; in obeying what the Church requires of us, but not as obedient to it: not to need the Church is the ultimate act of defiance, more ultimate even than Satan's, for the Church needs to be needed and Marguerite's freedom puts her beyond all need, whereas Satan needs God if he is to be Satan. And while the Church can easily expel from its ranks those who merely dissent from its teachings, for they confess the Church's role in the very act of dissenting, it cannot tolerate those who grant to the Church all truth and all virtue, but deny to it any character of necessity. For such an attitude renders the Church absolutely irrelevant.

True heresy, that is to say, is in one sense completely orthodox, in one sense absolutely indistinguishable from orthodoxy. It needs not deny anything that the Church proclaims as truth – except the Church which proclaims it. And it is, as I understand it, just this insight which lies at the source of those theological instincts from which has arisen that movement within Cambridge theology we have learned to call 'Radical Orthodoxy'. For Radical Orthodoxy – a movement with which I am myself unwilling to identify except in its grasp of this fundamental insight – is the protest of orthodoxy at the dominance of just that form of heresy which is represented by Marguerite Porete.

So let us shift historical perspective back to our own times and agendas. Today there is a conventional reading of late medieval 'mystical' heresy which sees it culturally and philosophically as a form of proto-modernism, and as in some way anticipating theologically a Reformation mentality, for it is read as the protest of individual conscience and experience – and sometimes more particularly as the protest of individual female conscience and experience – against the repressive claims of an authoritarian orthodoxy. As Karl Marx once put it, Luther laid the foundations of modernity by replacing the medieval faith in authority with the authority of individual faith. Fine. But none of this fits the case of Marguerite Porete, nor that of her near contemporary, the Dominican friar, Meister Eckhart, who suffered a similar, though less lethal, fate some eighteen years after Marguerite. Neither absolutizes 'the individual' in the manner so characteristic of 'modernity'; neither appeals to conscience against authority; neither would have been able to make any sense of modernist dualisms between the 'private' and the 'public', for both rejected its basis in distinctions of 'inner' and 'outer'. In fact, Marguerite's heresy is closer to what we have learned to call 'postmodernism' than to modernism, is closer to that mentality which refuses closure of any sort, whether in a medieval foundationalism of the Church, or in a modern foundationalism in an absolute individual selfhood. For our culture of postmodernism allows nothing to be given in any such wise that a secure edifice of knowledge, or any secure construction of desire and virtue, can be founded in an ultimate way upon it. For us, nothing is simply given; nothing is necessary, because everything is superfluous, everything is peripheral because nothing is centred. And paradoxically, because nothing holds at the centre there is no marginality either, and because nothing is necessary, nothing is excessive. Because, in other words, there can be no orthodoxy, heresy too is an impossibility.

I know these are dark words, but let me try and explain a little more clearly what I mean by saying that for our modern culture 'nothing is simply given'. There is a mentality of pure irony, a mentality which can say nothing unambiguously, nothing directly, but only slantingly, as it were, for it is a mentality of pure scepticism, a mentality which doubts not merely all capacity of the mind to settle in any truth, but doubts even all capacity to speak at all, for it is the mentality for which speech ceaselessly subverts itself, constantly destroying any purpose beyond itself. It is the mentality according to which in the end everything is, as it is put in some postmodern philosophies, a 'game', fun at the time, but as with all fun, only fun if it is as pointless as jokes are. For this mentality, there is therefore a degenerate sense in which everything is 'simply given': it is the sense in which a thing is simply given because it is pointless and without purpose, just there, brute, ultimately meaningless fact. It is the mentality, therefore, which possesses perfect lucidity, and, as for the perfect cynic, nothing is seen because everything lacks density and can be seen through; and because everything is seen through, there is never anything on the other side of anything at all: as these postmodernists put it, there are neither any 'foundations' on which truth can rest, nor any 'grand narrative' securing the mind in meaning and explanation.

It is this 'just there-ness', this brute and meaningless facticity to which the atheists appeal when challenged by the question: 'Then why is there anything at all, rather than nothing?' The question, atheists say, is meaningless: you can answer why this or why that, but as to the question, 'Why anything, and not nothing?' you just have to say: 'It's just there, that's all.' But do not deride the atheists.

They are close. Their mentality is so close to another mentality, and the difference between the two mentalities so subtle, and yet at the same time so ultimate that, I promise you in all seriousness, the whole fate of Western philosophical and theological culture depends upon getting that difference into some clear focus. It is the difference between two ways of saying that things are 'simply given'.

Let us try another tack. Let us do some terribly simple philosophy, terrible, because so much too simple for our over-educated minds readily to comprehend. Christians have from the earliest times maintained what we call the doctrine of 'creation *ex nihilo*' – 'out of nothing'. Now the imagination plays tricks with us here and we have to resort to subtler strategies than our imaginations possess if we are to outwit its ploys. I'll tell you – I think it is true – that much of this cathedral around us was 'made out of' Doulting stone. First there was a massy, formless rock down near the Bath, then there was some making and shaping and forming, and finally there was this magnificent capital of a man with a toothache, 'made out of stone'. We cannot think of any form of making which is not a making 'out of' something. So when we say that the world was made 'out of nothing' we have said something which, absolutely, and without qualification, we cannot think. Therefore, because we cannot think it, because we know that the expression 'made out of nothing' has stretched the idea of 'making' well beyond our comprehension, we begin instead to 'sort of' think, to imagine instead, to get a kind of analogy going between ordinary meanings of 'made out of' – for example, stone – and the unthinkable meaning of 'made out of nothing'. We begin to imagine the 'nothing' to be a kind of something that creation is made 'out of', we begin to think of 'nothing' as a sort of vague kind of 'primal soup', or, as Genesis does, as a sort of dark and still and formless 'deep'.

But we know this is wrong, we know that this is a sort of failure of thought, and that it is a sort of half-thinking in which we engage because we can scarcely bear the consequence that what we say when we talk of 'creation out of nothing' is actually quite unthinkable. Thomas Aquinas commented that the logic of the expression is actually straightforward: when we speak of 'creation out of nothing', he says, we should not think of 'nothing' as what creation is made out of, but rather that creation is a making of that completely incomprehensible kind where there is no 'out-of' involved at all. But note how close what follows from this is to the atheists' answer. For if this is what is meant by the Christian doctrine of creation, then it follows for the Christian also that when you look through creation, on the other side of it is, in strict truth, nothing. Creation rests on nothing whatever. Or you can say, can you not, as the postmodernist says, that creation is 'founded' on nothing whatsoever; or again you can say that there is no 'grand narrative', no story of creation which explains its process, for stories take and tell of time, and, as Augustine explained, there was no time in which creation occurred, because time is one of the things created. So we say, creation is set against the background of a vast emptiness – and there we go again imagining things, failing once again to accept the unthinkability of it all, because vastness and emptiness presuppose a huge container of space, and there is no space, no background, however empty, however huge, against which creation is set. 'Out of nothing'. No matter, no time, no space, no emptiness, no 'out of'. Utterly incomprehensible, dizzy-making, mysterious.

Or, as the atheists say: 'It's just there, a given, brute fact.' Well, is that what we are saying? No, we say, because though 'not out of' anything, still, it is *made*. And there, in that dark, opaque thought which is not a thought, in that sense of the 'madeness' of things which is beyond the grasp of all sense, a thought beyond thought which yet penetrates all our thought and experience of the world with a glimpse of its mystery, of its reality and truth lying beyond both it and beyond us, is the first, primitive, opaque awareness of a meaning we can attach to the name which is not a name, 'God', that name which Moses sought and was given, which named the face which Moses begged to see and was denied the sight of, because it was wrapped in a cloud, 'for no one may see my face and live'. This is the true 'darkness of God', which is nonetheless a light, a 'brilliant darkness', an excess of light, being like the flash of lightning too bright for the eye, plunging sight into deeper obscurity yet. This is the visibility of the Godhead which is an invisibility, a presence which is an absence, a mystery unutterably beyond us yet the foundation of our sensible, sensuous familiar world, present to us in that world in its character of being given by its maker.

And this is the second sense – our Christian sense – in which things are 'simply given', a Christian sense completely lost in the postmodern sense; for no longer for the Christian are things 'simply given' in the blank empty meaningless stare of some brute 'just-there-ness'; they are given in the sense that they are given to us, have the character of a gift. You won't recapture the vertiginous unthink-ability of this, however, in the recognition of creation's giftedness, until you see it in your own existence as such. For think of it: gifts are gifts not just when they are given, but only when they are also received. But if my existence – my being there rather than not-being there – is in the nature of a gift, don't forget that until I am given, I am not there to receive the gift. I am, my existence is, in a sense, pure gift; I am proud to say for this reason that I am, after all, indeed God's gift to the human race; it can make no sort of sense to say that I am God's gift *to me*. For, as Duke Vincentio says, in Shakespeare's *Measure for Measure*, 'Heaven doth with us as we with torches do, not light them for themselves'.

I think we can know this, just about, out of the resources alone of that rationality which is given to me in my existence. We can begin to guess, out of this dim and obscure acknowledgement of our giftedness – as it were, 'in a glass darkly' – that the meaning of this must lie somewhere in the significance of love. Perhaps we can guess at the possibility of an infinitely unconstrained love at work in this, for do not forget this *ex nihilo* even here. 'Out of nothing' . . . that is to say, there are no further purposes in creation, no reasons, no ulterior motives, nothing gained by it, nothing added by it, no profiteers. If God gives he gives out of sheer goodness, because, in a wonderful image of Meister Eckhart's, the divine goodness seethes and boils and overflows into creation as water heated in a pan, out of the sheer purposeless delight and enjoyment of goodness itself. And, as Thomas Aquinas says: *et ille est maxime liberalis*, he alone is absolutely free-handed, because, he adds, God acts without interest in any good he can do for himself, but out of the sheer joy of so acting – in short, this God always acts *ex nihilo*, out of nothing, gratuitously, graciously, for the joy of giving. Therefore, as wisdom says in Proverbs (8.31), she plays with the children of men because it is her delight to do so.

We might, in our own dim and obscure way, guess at this possi-bility for ourselves. But we could not know from any sources of our own that inner life of God, that riotously unconstrained free, seething goodness which is the deep abyss of the Godhead, and is the abyss of unmixed love, unless there were a giftedness more mysteri-ous even than the gift of our own being and existence itself; and that gift, on which our existence has no claim, is the gift of some share in the divine self-understanding, in God's own knowledge of his own love; and we are given that in the gift of his Son, for no one knows the Father except the Son. Our faith in Jesus Christ is a sort of participation, whereby our created existence is drawn into the very life of God, so that giver and gift share one life, one happiness, one joy: thus do we become by grace, that is to say, by gift, what God is by nature.

All this is to say but one thing: that because at that seething, boiling core of the divine being is a sort of 'play', so, through grace and faith, at the centre of our Christian life – it being through participation what the divine life is by nature – is also that same presence of the playful. You might think such an image to be a trivialization; for play is unserious, pastime stuff, what you do to relax when the important work of the day is done. And true enough: I would like you to attend to a very genuine reversal of assumption here: just consider how true play is simply for enjoyment; you play golf, if you are of such taste, for the enjoyment of golf: the enjoyment stops there in the golf itself, and even if you also play golf for a purpose, for profit of some sort, the enjoyment is in the golf, not in the profit. You read novels for the enjoyment of novels: and if you read them for an education, novels won't educate those who can't enjoy novels. You listen to Mozart so as to be seduced by the music, and those who can only be seduced for a purpose obviously know nothing of sex. And while I know there are serious people who will only play games to get fit – just as I once knew a serious person who tried to like Bach because he was ashamed of preferring Tchaikovsky – you simply do not understand games, or play, if you engage in them for any further purpose. The point of games is to be pointless. Just as the point of praying is to be pointless. The Dominican theologian Herbert McCabe once said that you do not understand prayer at all unless you can see that it is a complete waste of time. It is a complete waste of time as our existence is a complete waste of time; our existence is caught up in the divine play, because it has no point, no purpose, no utility: being thus simply the completely free outflow of the divine excess of love, being thus utterly gratuitous, being thus pure grace, our existence is well understood as gift. We are simply given.

But now again, see how very close this Christian perception of 'givenness' comes to the postmodern. There is a sense in which, whatever about some of its philosophical absurdities, the postmodern mentality is a genuinely welcome reaction against an excess of modern seriousness – as I should say, of a certain confluence of Protestant and capitalist seriousnesses. Think how, on the side of the capitalist mentality play is marginalized, because unproductive, and is retrieved for that mentality only in so far as it can be sucked back into the purposes of the market and productivity; and think of the corresponding, even, according to some, the reinforcing mentality of a certain kind of Protestantism – by no means, incidentally, confined within Protestant circles – which has stripped out of Christianity the mere joy of liturgical playfulness and the splendid uselessness of the contemplative life – what your Melvyn Matthews has called 'delighting in God' – on account of their pointlessness. For sure, what, in the postmodern mentality can seem – relative to that modern seriousness – a trivialization of existence and life is, in some sense at least, a pale recognition of a fundamental Christian truth which is utterly subversive of capitalist utility: that the point of things is to be useless, that the meaning of things is beyond meaning, because the meaning of things is love, and love knows only the good, and cannot coexist with the merely useful.

But if so close to one another, the postmodern and the Christian mentalities are, after all, utterly different, even opposed, as heresy is to orthodoxy. For the word 'heresy' is derived from the Greek word *hairesis*, which means 'choice'. In the good old days, when there was such a thing as an orthodoxy, the heretic was a picker and chooser of preferred truths; the heretic was an arbitrary person, who could not accept what was given because it was given, but accepted what was acceptable; for the heretic is the person who, as it were, always looks the gift-horse in the mouth. So, the heretic was a person who took a partial truth for the whole and distorted the whole in the name of the part. But today, I said, heresy is no longer a possibility, because orthodoxy is impossible. It is impossible because, today, you cannot choose a partial truth in spite of the whole, when the only truth acknowledged is choice itself. 'Choose your own truth.' The comedian Dave Allen used to end his television programmes with the blessing: 'And may your God go with you' – as if you could have any God you choose. And this is the postmodern heresy: the blessing is worthless, for 'your' God, being but yours, is bound to go with you, is bound to you by your choosing, because invented by your choosing, a petty little godlet of your own fabrication. In a world where everything is choice, everything is at once heresy and at the same time orthodoxy, at once 'yours' and at the same time unchallengeable. You can have any God you like so long as it is only the God that you like. You can even have the 'orthodox' Christian God – if you like.

For this postmodern mentality, therefore, everything is 'simply given', not in the sense that everything is 'gift', but in the sense that my freedom is the only explanation of everything; for this mentality, all creation is transparent, not because you can see through it to that abyss of its nothingness which is filled by the unknowable divine love, but with the transparency of my own, arbitrary, choosing; the world is not 'mine' because it is given to me, it is a mere 'given' which is 'mine' because there is nothing to explain it but what I choose should do so. The meaning of orthodoxy, in the end, is the meaning of gift; the meaning of heresy, in the end, is the meaning of choice. The meaning of orthodoxy, therefore, is the meaning of love, and the meaning of heresy is therefore the meaning of power. And the conflict between these two is the meaning of Jesus' life, the ultimate gift of love, which came into a world which knew only power. For which reason, the world had to reject that gift, had to kill Jesus, for to accept the Father's gift of his Son was to accept that that gift was all the meaning of all the world and that all the meaning of all the world is therefore that it is given not chosen, is found in love and not in power.

3

How to be 'Other': Enlightenment, Postmodernity and Mission

I gave this brief talk in April 1998 to a session of a conference in the University of Birmingham on 'Mission', held in honour of the great Anglican missionary bishop, Lesslie Newbigin. Some indication of how foolishly we academics can find ourselves agreeing to speak well beyond our competence can be seen in how quickly I bring the subject of mission in contemporary Western culture back into my familiar territory of the medieval, though not entirely without purpose. For it seems to me that there is often within the premodern traditions of Christian (also Jewish and Muslim) theology, a potential for a radicalism of thought unsuspected by our own contemporary culture, and capable of challenging it strangely, but persuasively.

It is with a sense of the irony of it that one notes how the fashion for the postmodern deconstruction of 'grand narratives' seems inseparable from its own particularly high level of generalization and periodization of history. Would we know how to describe 'postmodernity' if not in terms of 'modernity'? In that case, may we not ask how far postmodernism is compelled first to fabricate the monstrous philosophical and cultural monolith of 'modernity' in order then to deconstruct it? Well, one can ask, though the answer is by no means obvious, for of course there truly have been, and perhaps still are, 'modernists' who thought they belonged within a great progressivist story of unifying and enlightening reason. But even if that is so, there is too much unevenness, the record is far too patchy, too diverse and plural to generate anything but a very occasionally illuminating hypothesis out of so high-level a description of 'modernity' such as postmodernists so gleefully react to. In any case, there were always historiographers within that epoch who had no need of 'deconstruction' to be sceptical of that modernist story, having their own grounds for doing so; and in that same period of 'modernity' there were always philosophers, equally legitimate children of their times, who subverted the constructions of European rationalism, or who resisted its structuring dualisms, somehow miraculously without the assistance of a Derrida or a Deleuze.

For my part, as one who occupies a kind of philosophical ground within the territory of the theological, I have my doubts about some of the contemporary uses within theology of the generalized 'epochizations' of the postmodernist. In part this is simply a scepticism in principle of a vaguely empiricist sort. In other part, however, it is the less theorized scepticism of the medievalist who looks for signs of the 'modern' epoch from the other end in its origins, a scepticism which is informed by the evidence, particularly the evidence of religious history, which questions the explanatory value of the standard periodizations of the medieval and the modern and has difficulty identifying where, in the historical record, this 'modernity' is supposed to begin. I used to think that there was something to be gained from the exploration of analogies between postmodern deconstruction and some premodern theological deconstructions, particularly within the schools of negative mysticism. But since, on standard criteria for what counts as 'modernity', it is evident that modernity must have begun economically in Northern Italy in the twelfth century, politically in fourteenth-century France and theologically in the nominalisms of northern Europe in the same century, I do not see how we can work with those uniform periodizations which place 'modernity's' beginnings in the sixteenth century, or at any one time; and that at best only very limited comparative work is possible, between particular texts and literatures – perhaps between Derrida and Meister Eckhart. And whenever one does engage in such particular and local studies, every time it seems that epochal stereotypes of 'the modern', the premodern and the postmodern serve only to obscure their significance.

Well, then, if, as I do for the purposes of this discussion, we take it that among the central and urgent theoretical questions for a theology of mission within contemporary British society is the question, as one might put it grandiloquently, of 'the other' – the otherness of faiths and of unfaiths and of how a Christian faith might address its notions of mission to that plurality – then it might seem worthwhile for a medievalist like me to raise the question whether there is anything to be gained from the exploration of some medieval ideas of 'otherness' with reference to our preoccupations with 'the other' today; and so with the question of how the shape and form of dialogue with 'the other' is, for a Christian, very intimately tied into the shape and form of our constructions of 'otherness' itself. Forgive me for the very extremely abstract character of this proposal: but G. B. Shaw once wrote to *The Times* complaining that since he was too busy to write a short letter they would have to accept a long one, and he had a point: in addresses of such brevity as this one must be, the pressure of time enforces abstraction, suppression of detail and compression of thought.

Well, then, a few, very compressed, abstractions. It is often still supposed that the medieval world was characterized by a kind of theological and cultural uniformity and self-sufficiency which rendered it incapable of doing due justice to the 'otherness' of alternative, and rival, religious and cultural traditions. Part of this is a myth, unsupported by the evidence. In fact there is probably as much theological diversity in thirteenth-century Europe as there is in sixteenth-century Europe, moreover, across many of the same issues. What needs explaining is not why medieval theological uniformity gave way to early modern theological diversity, but why the theological conflicts of the sixteenth century resulted in schism and did not in the thirteenth. Nonetheless, medieval Christendom in all its diversity and internal 'othernesses' notoriously failed in different ways to meet any moral standard of dialogue with Jews and Muslims as living alternative cultures, just as it failed of moral adequacy in its practices for dealing with heresy. But this moral failure is probably as much a consequence of a conceptual failure which was in turn rooted in the limitedness of medieval experience of otherness. 'The cultural or religious other' in the medieval world was almost always treated on the model of the heretical, that is to say, on the model of betrayal: for the heretic draws upon the shared insights he or she possesses in common with the orthodox and then treacherously turns them against that common origin. The significant 'others' of the medieval age were of course, Jews and Muslims, both of whom it was possible to comprehend within this particular dialectic of heretical inclusion/exclusion in a way that, had they been a significant presence within the medieval Christian world, Hindus or Buddhists could never have been accommodated. And the one possibility of dissent from the standpoint of non-heretical and absolute denial, atheism, exists for the medieval theologian only as an intellectual hypothesis, not as a genuine cultural option, exhibited in an atheistic personal life-style or socially organized way of life, and so as no actual threat. In short, medieval 'otherness' is generally a category, as one might put it, of deviant inclusion, of fall-out within the family.

In this connection, you will perhaps note that it is now fashionable within the Roman Catholic Church to apologize for these historical failures: it has already done so, inadequately as many think, to the Jews and to Galileo; it appears to be about to do so, whether adequately or not, for the Crusades and the Inquisition, and so also to Muslims and heretics. But if one is entitled to a certain scepticism about the value of such historically retrospective remorse, it will be, among several different kinds of reason, at least for reasons of intellectual honesty on our part: it seems inconsistent, and not very honest, for us to condemn the past in its failures to respect the true 'otherness' of 'the other' when that moral outrage is itself a failure to acknowledge the 'otherness' of that past itself. We should not, whether morally or intellectually, seek to eat our cake and have it, for the pleasingly self-flattering advantage of moral high ground.

Besides, can we be sure that our 'dialectics of the other' today are any more sophisticated than the medieval, or are they, as I suspect, but mirror images of, inversions, of a like crudity? On the one hand, our contemporary relativisms are rooted in an abhorrence of inclusivist cultural imperialism, in a conception of radical 'otherness' which is, in my view, as logically preposterous as it is ecumenically unproductive. On the other hand they are exhibited in a naive theory of consensuality, which finds within the multiplicity of faith traditions a convergence upon some single, 'ultimate reality'; and, with all due respect to my illustrious predecessor, John Hick, this is a conception which hovers ambiguously between a liberal patronization of the otherness of the Buddhist and the epistemologically vacuous, or, conceivably, it is a bit of both.

And so, rather simple-mindedly, I ask you to consider whether contemporary theorists, including contemporary theologians, do not have much to learn from the dialectically far more complex notions of 'otherness' contained in the apophatic traditions of medieval mysticism: for a pseudo-Denys or a Meister Eckhart the otherness of God is both absolute and, for that very reason, absolutely accessible. Far from this conception of the otherness of God is the dualistic mentality of a Cupitt who is so trapped in the conceptions (yes, perhaps) of 'modernity', as to be able to conceive

of the transcendent otherness of God only as entailing a sort of
'crushing overagainstness', as an alienation, which squeezes all reality
out of creation, leaving him with but the one alternative of flatten-
ing out that transcendence into the immanence of a supposititious
neo-Buddhism. For the pseudo-Denys the transcendence of God is
to be found only on the other side of 'all similarity and difference',
thus defining that difference as so absolute as to be uncontainable
within our categories either of opposition or of identity; and in the
same tradition, Eckhart's God is the negation of the negation, the
opposing of oppositions, but not as reconciled, even 'ultimately
reconciled', in some higher synthesis. For, for Eckhart, there is no
knowable ultimate. For anything knowable is not ultimate and anything ultimate is unknowable. This God is not, therefore, to be
attained to in some syncretistic, knowable synthesis, but is placed in
utterly open space, an 'abyss', or a 'nothingness', he calls it, at once
beyond us and at the same time the 'ground' of our very selfhood,
and so as more intimately 'involved' in that selfhood than any
created 'other' could be. For the 'otherness' of God in such high
medieval theologies is such that it could not stand in any relation of
exclusion with anything whatever. Therefore, it is precisely *because
of* the absoluteness of the divine transcendence, not in spite of it,
that Augustine can speak of God as more intimate to me than I am
to myself.

Such notions disturb, tantalize with their radicalness, they tease
even our prophets of postmodern difference, even Derrida himself,
who appears not to know quite how to situate himself in relation to
them, unsure, as he now seems to admit, whether Eckhart is, or is
not, thereby postulating some forbidden, some insufficiently deconstructed 'hyperessential reality', or whether Eckhart is bidding him
towards some final deconstructed deconstruction, some final
promethean act of throwing down the idolatrous godlets alike of the
petty theists and petty atheists of our times. For if such radically
accessible radical otherness is vertiginously threatening to the easy
theists of our times – if they, of all faiths and traditions, can hardly
know what it is that they affirm when they call upon their God in
prayer or worship or theology – can it be any less subversive of the
atheists, whose acts of denial are placed equally beyond their reach?

I do not think I know what the task of mission is in contemporary
Britain – indeed I am sure that I do not – but I am sure that it cannot
lie within strategies which have abandoned that contestation with

an intellectual culture which is possessed only of idols, whether complacently to affirm them or with equal complacency to deny them. Ecumenism, inter-faith dialogue, dialogues between faith and our theologically unchallenged culture are, I suppose, the first, if not the only strategies of mission today. But if no one should suppose that it consists in nothing else, I do not conceive of any mission today achieving any degree of adequacy which does not pose a radical intellectual challenge to the pretentiously self-sufficient claims of our cultures, theistic of any faith or atheistic and of none, to know: whether the claim is to know, as the modernist thinks, the rational key to all things, or, even, as the postmodernist thinks, to know the difference. For beyond the sameness of modernity, beyond the difference of postmodernity, beyond the oneness of Islam and the trinity of the Christian, beyond the affirmation of the theist and the denial of the atheist, lies the subversive cloud of unknowing, undoing all our knowing, unknowing all our doing, an edge and horizon of mystery which at once surrounds and sustains all and challenges all, is at once indescribable and subversive of all our descriptions, an abyss, as Eckhart puts it, into which we must sink, 'out of something into nothing'.

4

Postmodernism and Christian Faith

This sermon was delivered at Evensong in the chapel of Pembroke College, Cambridge, in October 2001. The underlying theme is common to a number of other pieces and is that of an intellectual cynicism, or more generally, the cynical corruption of intellect which I perceive as characterizing the 'postmodern' mentality. For this mentality, to see everything is to see nothing, because all seeing is 'seeing through' to the 'other'. It is ultimately a nihilistic mentality, for of course, only 'nothing' is on the other side. There is, apparently, little enough to distinguish this mentality from the Christian perception that all things are created ex nihilo, and so, in a sense for the Christian too there is only 'nothing' on the other side of 'everything'. Except this difference which is the whole difference: that for the postmodern, the world is simply given; for the Christian, the world is simply gift. The Christian and the postmodern are inversions of one another. The mirror image of 'nothing' accounting for things is love accounting for things. Both see the world as equally 'gratuitous', but in opposed senses.

Once in a queue for coffee at an academic conference I overheard a philosopher say, in comment upon a particularly clear paper we had just sat through: 'Thank God for lucidity, for at least you can see what's there.' 'Thank God for opacity', replied his companion, 'otherwise there is nothing to see.' Postmodernism, for all the density, obscurity – not to say obscurantism – of the prose in which so many of its advocates write, is, I should say, rather a cult of absolute transparency. It often proclaims itself as the mode of the ironic. But one might also think that it is the mentality of the perfect cynic, the mentality of one for whom, by virtue of the perfect transparency of all things – because nothing possesses any density – nothing is seen because everything is seen through.

I was asked by the Dean to speak to you today about postmodernism and Christian faith – for just a few minutes in a sermon. And I am not so sure that there is such a thing as a sermon about postmodernism which could avoid addressing the apparent contradiction contained within the conjunction. For the claims of postmodernism as a critical, ironic mode of thought and the claims of the sermon as at least for some an explication of Christian faith as truth, may seem to conflict. As, indeed, I think they do. For the postmodernist will permit the sermon on the strict condition that its claims upon our minds are disallowed in any absolute way. And though I should make no absolute claims for my sermon, I should think myself as justified in preaching at all only in acknowledgement of the words of Jesus, that we are not to call ourselves teachers (as it were in our own right) but only in service to a truth which belongs to us all, a truth which is our common possession, a truth which is not 'ours' in some sense (if there is a sense to it) in which it is a truth just 'for us', but a truth our minds and wills and hearts are judged by. For we are to speak of what we know, a gospel and a grace, whose claims upon our minds' service are absolute.

Of course, the postmodernists permit my sermon, but only as a discourse. They thus refuse it the character of a sermon. They see through its claims to offer firm grounds of truth, permitting only a standpoint: those claims have no foundational character, no ultimacy, for the postmodern mentality is that of the ultimacy only of the penultimate, or, as they will sometimes put it, of the endless post-ponement of meaning and of judgement. In that sense, the post-modern mentality is one of total transparency: there is always something on the other side of everything, a something which can itself be deconstructed into its otherness. So in its perfect light, there is nothing which is simply seen.

As you can see, I take the postmodern mentality to be one in which intellectually everything is permitted; from which it would seem to follow that nothing can be required except that nothing can be required. Of course, it does not follow that this mentality cannot be challenged; in fact, I suppose, there is every reason to ask whether the postmodern mentality cannot itself be deconstructed: at the very least it can be asked to explain itself. And after all, it would seem not very difficult to account for the existence and persistence of this mentality in the Northern part of the world, when one considers the cultural, political, economic and military soil in which it has grown and in which it thrives.

For is it a very puzzling thing that postmodernism should originate in a continent which has experienced the quantities of military violence and slaughter that has Europe in the twentieth century; which has visited political, economic and military devastation upon so many other parts of the world; which for half of that century relied upon the quite manic defence strategy of what it called 'mutually assured destruction'; which was able to permit that systematic extermination of races and peoples and 'minorities' which we now call 'ethnic cleansing'; which has relied upon a form of economy which visits devastation upon the economies of the South and tests to near destruction its own natural environment? It is scarcely puzzling if a continent whose recent history is of such a character should gaze into the mirror of its experience and declare itself to be 'postmodern', as describing, to use Marx's account of such ideologies, 'the natural and spontaneous mode of thought' of such an age.

But while that might not be strange, there is some paradox to be found in the curious failure of self-awareness of this ideology. Or perhaps it is not so paradoxical, perhaps it is natural and unsurprising that an ideology which declares there to be 'no foundations' anyway should, in consequence, be systemically incapable of acknowledging its own foundations; that it should be, in a certain spiral of self-ignorance with which Freud was so familiar, utterly incapable of recognizing the need to deconstruct deconstruction itself back into the forces – economic, cultural, political – outside itself from which derive its own naturalness and spontaneity. I suppose I simply (and naively) mean: when it comes to deconstruction, two can play at that game.

That said, the game is still somewhat too easily played. After all, I know Christians who think there are theological prospects in playing on the postmodern side of it, and it is easy to see why they might be tempted to suppose this. I read some Heidegger the other day (I confess that it was duty to some students rather than inclination which had me doing this) and I found him making a distinction between what he called 'beings' and their 'ground'. Roughly, what he appeared to mean by this distinction is what I had in mind when distinguishing between what you see – beings, objects in the world – and the light in which you see them – what he calls 'being'. Now, of course, light itself is invisible; it is only when light is refracted by an object it sets upon that you can see it, and then it is not the light precisely which you see, but what is lit. So, the light by which we see is not, and cannot be, an object of sight: beings, we know, but being we do not.

Now when I read this in Heidegger, I was struck by its resemblance to the words of an author more familiar to me, the thirteenth-century Franciscan master of theology, St Bonaventure, who said the same, only of God. It is within the divine illumination, he said, that we know the world of objects and things. But the divine light itself always escapes our vision: try to make God into an object of our sight, and he disappears as the light, becomes just another object, and so disappears as God, who is always other than what we can see. For this reason, Bonaventure says, it is the invisibility of the divine light which is the cause of the visibility of creatures, and so appears to us as if the 'darkness of God'. And if you had asked Bonaventure on what sort of scriptural foundation he rested this sort of reflection, he would undoubtedly have offered a verse from the first of today's readings: 'And Moses hid his face, for he was afraid to look at God' (Exodus 3.6); as also others from Exodus, most typically Yahweh's warning to Moses that 'my face you may not see, for no one may see my face and live' (Exodus 33.20).

Now Heidegger's conception of 'being' as the unknowable 'ground' of our knowledge of 'beings' was explicitly non-theological. But he was well aware that where he got it from was explicitly theological: it was from the writings of the fourteenth-century Dominican theologian, Meister Eckhart. So listen to these powerfully deconstructive words of Eckhart – preached, may I say, in a sermon:

> God, who has no name – who is beyond names – is inexpressible, and the soul in its ground, which is God, is also inexpressible as he is inexpressible . . . [for] there is something above the created being of the soul, and which is untouched by any createdness, which is to say nothingness . . . it is a strange land and a desert, and it is more without a name than nameable, more unknown than knowable . . .

Why do I call these words 'deconstructive'? Because in that ironic, self-subversive, manner of the deconstructionist, Eckhart tells us that the ground of our selfhood is the divine ground, so that, as it were, our centre is outside us, we are 'decentred' beings. But he also tells us that that divine ground on which we are centred denies to us any secure ultimacy of the kind which might be thought to exist in some ultimate, given, knowable object on which all is founded. For as our centre is not a centre, so our ground is not in that sense a ground in which it is a solid, known, foundation on which selfhood, or knowledge, or desire can rest. In relation to our knowledge of objects, of the world, God is always beyond, always other, always, as we might say, postponed. Why? Because to suppose God to be an object is always idolatrous: 'for no one may see my face and live'. The light in which we see is always other than what we can see in it.

So it is not hard to understand why some Christians might be tempted to explore their faith by means of a deconstructive strategy. And for sure, thus far, one is but exploring the relatively safe territory of the acknowledged premodern sources of much postmodern thought – acknowledged, after all, not merely by Martin Heidegger, but also by the high priest of postmodernism, Jacques Derrida. And it is true that there are symmetries: the distinctively Christian teaching of the creation of all things *ex nihilo*, 'out of nothing', is to be sure, the recognition that, in respect of its existence, there is only nothing – that is to say, there is not anything – which accounts for the world; it is absolutely gratuitous, nothing by way of antecedent conditions explains it; that though each thing within the world is explicable by reference to something else – we call that knowledge 'science' – that there is anything at all is not, and cannot be, explained in reference to anything we know of. And so, in a sense, it is a truth which Christians acknowledge that there are 'no foundations'.

And yet it is a foolish Christian who cannot see that the symmetries between the deconstructions of a postmodernist and of a negative theologian are mirror-images of one another, inversions, reversals. For the fierce light of postmodern deconstruction dissipates the natural solidities of the world into their differences, evacuates substance into otherness, alterity, always alterity. Whereas the light in which the Christian sees revises the gratuity of things as grace, it reframes postmodern arbitrariness as the giftedness of all things – for since nothing requires that there should be anything at all, that there is what there is seems now to be willed, to have the inexplicability of an unknowable, creative love. Hence, that light of Christian faith – itself a gift beyond our power – sees the being of all things as given to them, as theirs incomprehensibly to possess. We cannot see the light itself in which creation appears to us thus. But if it were not for that density, the opacity of our being – if that light were not refracted off our created existence – then there would be nothing to see, we would know nothing of our giftedness, nor anything of the love which gives it.

For the Christian, of course, the revelation of this divinely arbitrary gift of love is completed in the Father's gift of his Son in Jesus Christ, an act of supreme incomprehensibility which but deepens the incomprehensibility of creation. For, as again Bonaventure tells us, the full visibility of that light which creation refracts back on the Father is resumed in the human nature of Christ. But it is in the paradox of the destruction of that human nature on the Cross, that divine entry into the darkness of sin, that we are finally drawn into the full light of faith, which is our entry into the unfathomable, and if you like 'foundationless', mystery of the *Deus absconditus*, the depths of the Father's love.

Which is why, I suppose, that in that other of today's readings Jesus tells us: 'I, when I am lifted up from the earth, will draw all people to myself' (John 12.32).

Politics, Piety and the Church

5

Amos, Justice and the Knowledge of God

I gave this talk in a series on BBC Radio 4 on the prophets of the Hebrew Scriptures in Lent, 1986. Not long after, I ceased to describe myself publicly as a Marxist, and would not now think of myself in such terms as would appear to provoke a crisis of consistency between a Marxist and a Christian commitment. On the other hand, I continue to owe much more to the mind of that great thinker (and inept revolutionary) than is now fashionable to admit to, and though less noisily and moralistically intolerant than I then was of a Christian practice immature in its 'political' commitments, I should still want to maintain, as fundamental to Christian practice, the theological proposition that 'knowing God is' (or at least is inseparable from) 'doing justice'. I learned how to recover that connection, so obvious to Amos, from the Third World theologies of liberation in the 1970s and 1980s. But just how fundamental to Christian (and of course Jewish) practice that proposition is, is shown by what Amos knows is entailed by it: that injustice to, or simply blind neglect of, the poor, harnessed to religious piety, is a form of idolatry. And that is still worth saying.

I hate, I despise your feasts, and I take no delight in your solemn assemblies. Even though you offer me your burnt offerings and cereal offerings, I will not accept them, and the peace offerings of your fatted beasts I will not look upon. Take away from me the noise of your songs; to the melody of your harps I will not listen. But let justice roll down like waters, and righteousness like an everflowing stream. (Amos 5.21–24)

Were I to choose just one text, any text at all, which pulled together the loose and various strands of my own commitments, religious and political, that bitter denunciation of Amos would probably be the one I would have to choose. I am, I think, a Marxist. I wish to be a Christian. Amos, of course, was neither. But Christianity, Marxism and the prophetic tradition in which Amos stands have cut deep into the tissue of the religious instincts of humankind and have exposed a raw nerve. It is a nerve which cries out, with the pain of an acknowledged hypocrisy, the most subtle and damaging hypocrisy there can be. It is the hypocrisy of the religious alibi for human exploitation, the hypocrisy of a pious neglect of the concerns of the poor, of those poor whom our wealth impoverishes and oppresses. Amos does not say merely that though we are pious we have neglected the poor. He says, rather more disturbingly, that we are pious so as not to notice that our comforts, indeed our very piety, depend upon their poverty:

> They sell . . . the needy for a pair of shoes – they . . . trample the head of the poor into the dust of the earth, and turn aside the way of the afflicted . . . they lay themselves down by every altar upon garments taken in pledge, and in the house of their God they drink the wine of those who have been fined. (Amos 2.6b–8)

I say that for myself, I am some sort of Christian and some sort of Marxist. Of course, that is about as absurd a proposition intellectually and in practice as it is possible to get. At any rate, it is so regarded in Britain. For that reason, it is also a painfully isolating one, for being a Marxist places me on the very margins of my Church, exposed and suspect. The Vatican has seen to that. And being a Christian distinctly lowers my credibility rate with Marxists. The isolation is ironical, for both Christianity and Marxism are movements to belong to. They are movements within which to explore and create radically new ways in which human beings can belong to one another, but because they appear to exclude one another, because both seem trapped within their own sense of mutual hostility, I can feel included by neither, at any rate, not fully. And sometimes I have to say I do long to be elsewhere than in this insular, narrow, and so easily scandalized world of British religious and political life, to be where the meeting of those two solidarities is no mere academic proposition, but a lived experiment and an experiment in living. In short, I sometimes wish to be in Latin America. But that is an idle fantasy. I belong here.

Self-pity being out of place, I come to the matter of prophecy. I know I am not either a fashionable Christian or a fashionable Marxist, but does that make me a prophet or does it just make me a novelty, a self-made eccentric? For tempting as it may be to think of oneself as a voice crying in the wilderness, is it not just possible that after all, the wilderness is in the voice. For I am but an academic. Professionally, I like no place better than the seminar, unless it be the study, and the study is the very workshop of fantasy and dottiness, where the merely academic synthesis seems fine on paper, and never mind the 'real world'. Moreover, temperamentally I am unsuited. We academics are a slow, hesitant, indecisive breed, and as we are trained to doubt everything we read, so often we learn to read ourselves sceptically and without confidence. And what is worse, we academics pay an exceedingly low price for our eccentricities. No one has ever paid me the compliment of persecution for my opinions. Far from it, I seem to be a rather popular choice among groups, whether of Christians or of Marxists, to give talks, read papers, write for their journals. With me, it is talk, talk, talk in a world in which to say everything is to do nothing. Even when I speak I am not heckled, nor when I have spoken do I receive abusive mail. I cannot remember anyone even being much angered by what I have said. No, I, at least, am no prophet. Self-doubt, of course is not confined to academics. The prophets themselves had their share of it. We make them out to be singular people, exceptional geniuses of the Spirit, but that was hardly Amos's view of himself:

> I am no prophet, nor a prophet's son; but I am a herdsman, and a dresser of sycamore trees, and the Lord took me from following the flock, and the Lord said to me, 'Go, prophesy to my people Israel.' (Amos 7.14–15)

What is more, Jesus himself had a rather downbeat view of what the Old Testament prophets had going for them:

> many prophets and kings desired to see what you see, and did not see it, and to hear what you hear, and did not hear it.' (Luke 10.24).

Christians, in other words, have no excuses, no alternatives. We are all prophets. This is evidently a business in which there are no experts anyway, so it is no excuse for you and me that we are not. Or to put it in another way, to think of prophecy as being for exceptional people, *is* our excuse. Being unexceptional ourselves, we conclude that we have none of the responsibilities of a prophet.

Well, Christianity in this country is quite astoundingly unprophetical, and I think Amos can tell us why. At any rate, he has told me in my own case. What Amos has to say is so startlingly clear, that naturally we don't see it at all. It is that if we imagine that we can somehow enter into the mystery of the Godhead through our worship, without first entering into the mystery of human oppression and poverty, and there taking sides unambiguously with the poor, then ours are not the mysteries of the divine, they are but the mystifications of injustice. To be in a false relationship with the poor is to be in a false relationship with God. If, Amos insists, we do not seek God within the search for justice, whatever we find, and whatever we end up worshipping, it will not be God:

'Behold the days are coming,' says the Lord God, 'when I will send a famine on the land; not a famine of bread, nor a thirst for water, but of hearing the words of the Lord. They shall wander from sea to sea, and from north to east; they shall run to and fro, to seek the word of the Lord, but they shall not find it.' (Amos 8.11–12)

And it was no different for Jesus. What was the sign he gave that his teaching was of God? Was it that men and women of power, prestige and wealth had received the Good News with joy? On the contrary, what Jesus had to say to the rich was extremely bad news about the great difficulty they would have even in understanding what he *meant* by his kingdom and its justice. It was to the poor that what Jesus preached was good news. And what of us? Ours, is it not, is the opposite experience, of getting rather further with the rich than with the poor, a fact which raises some questions about the class alliances of our churches. And if Amos is right, then the point is this: we cannot really be succeeding, even with the rich, if we are failing with the poor, even if we are filling some churches with the one and hardly any with the other. And, if Amos is right, then the false position our Christian communities are in will show up in the unreal character of their worship. And are not our solemn assemblies in some ways travesties, not, I realize, consciously hypocritical, but all the worse for being places of unconscious fantasy and delusion? It is, after all, at our liturgical assemblies, at our introverted, merely churchy fellowship, that Amos points the finger. And did Marx hate such Christian assemblies any more than Amos did, or for any different reason, namely that in and through them we are enabled to evade the choices which our unjust world thrusts upon us, by spiritualizing them into the empty gestures of a pious rhetoric?

> Therefore because you trample upon the poor and take from him exactions of wheat, you have built houses of hewn stone, but you shall not dwell in them; you have planted pleasant vineyards, but you shall not drink their wine. (Amos 5.11)

I admit that our Christian worship pays lip service to the rhetoric of social concern. We have acquired the liturgical accents of an ill-understood liberationism. We do, at least, pray for peace, with confidence when wars are elsewhere, though I seem to remember that we did so with rather more precious delicacy during the Falklands War. It was important to pray only rather imprecisely for the Argentinian dead; to have been too explicit would have been perhaps more divisive than our unstable parish unities could bear. For let us admit it, we Christians are paralysed by the harsh realities of the economic and political world. We infinitely prefer the consolations of our own warm-hearted fellowships. We know very well that to face up to the real issues of injustice in their political and economic dimensions would expose and rip apart that fellowship, and yet we know that we cannot simply ignore those real issues. And so we lapse into the style and practice of the rhetorical gesture at them. We are explicit enough to convince ourselves that we are open to the world, vague enough that we don't disturb each other's sensitivities. Thus it is that we pray and act in frozen postures of concern without action, for abstractions like 'peace' with 'justice for the unemployed', for 'handicapped people'.

And as for handicapped people, I, too, have played my part in parish group meetings, for example, to arrange rotas for transporting them to church. That is no problem, but how the atmosphere was changed when at one such meeting the question was raised as to why a severely disabled person was having to share a room in a local authority home. A brave soul ventured to suggest that cuts in public expenditure had something to do with it. 'But we cannot discuss that,' came the instant reply, 'that would be politics, and politics divides the parish.' Well, it would have been politics and it would have divided the parish. I am reminded of the remark of the Brazilian bishop, Dom Helder Camara, 'When I feed the hungry, they call me a saint. When I ask why they are hungry, they call me a communist'. Amos was an ordinary, plain Israelite. We are ordinary and plain, but he became a prophet because he responded without evasion to the dishonest religiosity of his people. He didn't fear to divide, and I do not see why we should fear the divisions which might result from a hard experience of learning.

Six years ago, I lived through the experience of a Church learning to take up the real problems of injustice, of racism, unemployment, bad housing and so forth, at the National Pastoral Congress of the Catholic Church in Liverpool. It had been my task to edit into a diocesan report for the Congress the work of parish group discussions. It was a shock to discover the implicit racism of some of those reports. I was scandalized by the naked self-interest contained in the support one group gave for nuclear deterrence simply on the grounds that many of its members were employed by the Ministry of Defence. I don't say that their attitudes make answers easy, on the contrary, the easiest thing is for us to go on, finding a way of being Christian which enables us to forget the problem, but Amos has blocked that way out:

> Woe to you who desire the day of the Lord! Why would you have the day of the Lord? It is darkness, and not light, as if a man fled from a lion, and a bear met him; or went into the house and leaned with his hand against the wall, and a serpent bit him. Is not the day of the Lord darkness, and not light, and gloom with no brightness in it? (Amos 5.18–20)

It will be a costly thing for Christians to pay the price of a faith committed openly to its role in the cruel, uncertain worlds of politics and economics. And yet for Amos, it is the price we must pay if we are truly to find our God. Before, therefore, we address ourselves to the tasks which such a commitment implies, there is a message which comes to us from the Church in parts of the Third World. It is that if we need consolation of any sort, it will be only such as can be found in that fine remark of the English Dominican, Herbert McCabe, 'that if we do not love we are scarcely alive, but if we do love, we will be killed'.

6

How to Kill People

In, I think, 1992, when visiting the United States for a conference, I was invited by a friend and former colleague Lyndon to stay with him for a few days at his new home in Atlanta, Georgia. 'But you will have to sing for your supper', he added, explaining that among his duties as the Director of an adult education centre attached to the Archdiocese of Atlanta, he had to organize the speakers for the monthly meetings of a rather exclusive club of senior business executives. He was short a speaker for that month and would I, by any chance, have a twenty-minute talk up my sleeve?

I rather too readily agreed to this condition, for it was only when I had done so that my friend explained a little more. 'They meet for lunch', he said, 'in an exceedingly expensive club and you give your talk before the food starts and answer their questions during the meal. Nothing too radical, mind,' he added (remembering that I had a Marxist past), 'they are very right-wing, and easily upset by anything left-wing.'

Well, I like a challenge, but I also know about hospitality and good-behaviour as a guest; and even if such things had not mattered to me, I knew very well how much they mattered to Americans from the southern states particularly, and I was in a quandary. For frankly, I am not at ease with those forms of Christianity which somehow contrive to combine the untroubled possession of immense wealth and power with the gospel message, or that of the Psalms or Amos, which all speak of the very great difficulty of doing any such thing. Anyhow, I quickly prepared a twenty-minute talk, as honestly as I could, on the subject of taking life and causing death, a subject on which my own views are as suitably pro-life and conservative as could be hoped for in the circumstances. My conscience would not, however, leave me entirely at ease with altogether avoiding the issue of wealth and power, and so I threw in a few little arrows of discomfort, I suppose as much to pacify my own conscience as seriously to trouble theirs.

As it happened, my mind was quickly diverted from my own moral dilemmas by a more immediate problem. 'What is the title of your talk?' Lyndon asked me. 'Hedgehogs', I replied. 'Hedgehogs, and How to Kill People'. 'Oh dear', said Lyndon, or something else robuster. 'They won't know what hedgehogs are, they don't have them in the States. You had better tell them about porcupines or ground-hogs or something else', *kindly omitting to comment that in any case hedgehogs are hardly the most suitable topic for conversation over lunch.*

As to my principles, I am not sure I stuck with them. But I stuck with my hedgehogs, merely glossing that they are like little porcupines and proceeded with my talk otherwise unamended by theological or moral scruple. And this is the talk I gave them.

I ought to begin by saying how very grateful I am to you all for inviting me to join you today, how honoured I am to be invited to help with your proceedings. In the Middle Ages – indeed still today – it was the practice in monasteries to eat in silence and listen to improving reading. In my limited experience of monastic food, there is rarely much on the menu to distract from the spiritual diet. Not so today; for this splendid hospitality, my thanks. But you must admit that, in some ways, you make good thought the harder by the splendour of these arrangements. We academics believe ourselves to be an ascetical breed, and are accustomed to think best when lean and hungry.

Or is it really true that your hospitality makes good thought harder? It is an ancient Catholic tradition, inherited from our Jewish origins, not just to welcome the stranger with a meal, but to put the eating of meals at the very centre of the mysterious life of the Church. It was by what he did at his last meal that Jesus said he wished to be remembered. He even said once, or possibly more than once, with that instinct for the startling comparison, that he himself was food and that, when we remembered him, it should be at a meal and one at which we should eat him. Unforgettable. So perhaps it is not so difficult, after all, to remember that here and now.

And this idea that we best celebrate the mystery of Christ by eating meals is not irrelevant to our subject today, which is to be about saving lives and caring for the dying: a Catholic perspective. Our time is limited and there is no possibility that we could deal in any detail with the issues, of agonizing difficulty and complexity, which we all know arise here. And so I will talk about the perspectives, the broad lines of thought, within which, as Catholics, we are invited to think these issues through. It is at this level that Jesus' partiality for meals is, as was everything he did and said, very revealing; for though he gave us no helpful moral advice on what, after all, are some very contemporary issues, he did offer us some perspectives which powerfully aid our consciences as we seek the solutions to them. I shall try to explain in what way this is so at the end of this talk. In the meantime, as a way of getting into the issues, let me start with another, I am afraid not very appetizing, illustration.

Let me tell you all that I think I know about hedgehogs. I was much put out to hear, just before we sat down, that you probably do not know what hedgehogs are, for I gather you do not have them in the United States. Well, they are rather like small porcupines in being prickly, but are quite unlike porcupines in reputation, for hedgehogs have a rather cuddly image in Britain, and figure as somewhat endearing creatures in children's literature, the most famous such beast being a certain 'Mrs Tiggywinkle'. Also, I do not know whether porcupines hibernate, whereas the point of my mentioning hedgehogs in our connection is that they do.

Now as you will know, in order to hibernate effectively, an animal must reduce its body temperature to a very precise degree, above that of extinction and below that at which it is stimulated into activity – you can imagine that six months of insomnia would be an unsatisfactory way to pass a winter, even for a hedgehog.

I believe that hedgehogs are social animals and like to hibernate in groups, or at least in pairs. This is because they do not have a very efficient biological mechanism for reducing their body temperature to the exact required level and so they depend upon a certain sort of cuddly co-operation to get that temperature right. They adjust the distance between each other during hibernation so that they are not too close, for then excessive warmth would overstimulate them into wakefulness. Nor must they be too far from each other, for then they would freeze each other out. Now you can see that if hedgehogs do not have a very efficient biological mechanism for regulating temperature they must have a very efficient social mechanism for getting it right: they know, by instinct, how to get the distance between themselves exactly right so as thereby to regulate the temperature to the appropriate level.

'Getting the distance right'. It was the German philosopher of the nineteenth century, Artur Schopenhauer, who used the hibernating hedgehogs as a sort of parable for human morality. Human morality, he thought, is a matter of learning how to get the distances between us exactly right. You can see how this works out in all sorts of instances and from them you can see another thing: how appropriate distances between human beings vary a lot from one situation to another and how we have to regulate those distances by the human power of judgement – not, as hedgehogs do, by instinct.

A mother will stay very close to her infant child. But if, as the child grows up, she fails to allow that distance to increase, then the child will not grow up. As I am sure you know, the problem most adolescents have with growing up is not that they do not want to but that their parents are reluctant to let them; and that is generally because the parents don't want to grow up themselves into a new, adjusted relationship of distance. Hence they smother their children.

Another example: first-year students in my university generally call me 'Dr Turner'. In their second year they generally call me 'Denys'. Somewhere between these two they avoid calling me anything at all, because their relationship with me lies in that awkward hinterland between two distances, symbolized by first name and surname modes of address. Americans first-name in a way which can be quite startling to an English person who is not used to it; but then we are by repute a little distant and stand-offish and Americans are quite extraordinarily friendly, as I know so very well from personal experience. In our two cultures we relate socially with different judgements of distance.

So, learning how to judge the right distance, appropriately for different circumstances is, Schopenhauer thought, a good part of what human morality is about. Too close, and we smother each other, too distant and we freeze each other out. But now to the point. Let us get onto the subject of killing.

Let me tell you how to kill people efficiently; or rather, here's how to get yourself, and, if you are in the business of doing so, here's how to get others, to kill people. First, you have got to call your proposed victims names. Note, in this connection, that practically no species of animal, with the exception of female Black Widow spiders and human beings, regularly engage in the killing of members of their own kind. A black rat will not kill another black rat, but is a rampant slayer of brown rats. On the other hand, if you inject a black rat with the odour of a brown rat, then, because it doesn't smell right, the unfortunate black rat becomes vulnerable to the aggression of its own kind. For it is by smell that rats identify members of their own species.

Now what the laboratory experimenter does chemically to the black rat, human beings do to each other by means of language. Normally, we are biologically inhibited from killing other humans for just so long as we recognize them as belonging to our own kind. So if we propose to kill a fellow human being and justify it, we have to redescribe him in such a way that he no longer belongs to us, becomes an alien being who doesn't smell right, and in that way the inhibition against killing is effectively weakened.

We can see this in times of war. I am sorry to say that when my country went to war to retrieve the Falkland/Malvinas Islands, some of our newspapers fell to describing Argentinians as 'Argies', 'Wops' and worse things besides. And I am sorry to say that when you set your young people upon the armies of North Vietnam, you fell to calling North Vietnamese 'Gooks' who, I once heard General Westmoreland say, can be killed with the less scruple because they have an 'Eastern' attitude to death and to the value of human life. I make no moral judgement about either war. I merely point to a fact: that human beings cannot be got to kill other human beings without degrading them first verbally. We need to do this if we are to justify what we propose to do by persuading ourselves that our victims are not quite, not strictly, not fully, human. So we find the name which says that they are not. Perhaps, then, the least true truism of all is that only sticks and stones break bones, but that names they cannot harm me: for if we propose to kill each other we must first humiliate each other verbally. Otherwise, we cannot get ourselves to do it.

To put it in other, hedgehogly, words, we will allow ourselves to kill only those whom we have set at a maximum distance from ourselves by means of that most powerful of human tools, the power of misdescription. We deny our victims any community with ourselves, we deny that there is any community we share, we attempt to affirm our own humanity in the act of denying our victim his.

What occurs in war occurs in some practices in some hospitals and in many abortion clinics. Again, I will stick to facts, and will not pass moral judgements. For sometimes we do this truthfully, sometimes with falsehood and self-deception. We think that if you can truthfully say that a comatose person is in a persistent and irreversible 'vegetative' state, then you are justified in turning off a ventilator; but if we cannot truthfully redescribe the person as a vegetable, then we would not be justified in doing this. Is the foetus a parasite on its mother's body, a person with as yet unrealized potential, a potential person, or what? These are not merely 'matters of words', for words are never 'mere': by words we set others at distances from one another and our judgements of distance license us, or do not license us, we think, to kill.

So the question is: who or what belongs to us? Who, or what do we name by that same name by which we call ourselves? And notice here how radically different is Jesus' answer to that question from the answer which is likely to be given by what he called 'the world'. Jesus' answer is given in parables, parables which are the foundation of a truly Christian approach to the question of our attitudes to death and dying. And, those parables were most usually parables of eating meals.

The Gospels tell us very little about the personal life of Jesus, about his likes and dislikes, for that is not their purpose. But occasionally we get a glimpse, incidentally, of his personality and I think one thing you can certainly say about Jesus is that he was an enthusiastic party-goer. Jesus regarded a good meal as so important a symbol of the life he wished us to live that he was prepared to risk his good name for the sake of a party; in particular he gained a reputation among his critics for being quite indiscriminate in the selection of the company he was prepared to keep.

He told stories about parties, about good ones and bad. He was not always an ideally polite guest himself, and on one occasion he was prepared to be quite openly critical, and to his face, of his host's hospitality; but above all, as I say, there was his rather peculiar attitude to the matter of the guest list, a subject on which he was quite unprepared to give a fig for normal standards of compatibility between those he thought you should invite. He himself was unhappy at exclusive gatherings but obviously enjoyed the company of ex-prostitutes, reformed corrupt revenue officials, ex-terrorists and unpopular foreigners of different religions. On one occasion he told approvingly of a party which truly scraped the bottom of the barrel, a party to which were invited only passers-by. And on that occasion he explained the one condition that he insisted upon, namely that his guests should recognize that they were sinners: one guest was bounced, if you remember, for not wearing the required dress.

Now all Jesus' parables are meant to explain something about what he called his 'kingdom', a metaphor which in republican America must have a rather quaint ring to it. Most particularly, Jesus' stories about parties have that meaning, for they were intended to indicate who belongs to his kingdom. If that is so, then his message is very clear: the people who will find themselves most easy and at home in the kingdom are people at the end of their tether, people in whom their humanity has been reduced nearly to zero, oppressed as they are by circumstance, or by their own mistakes, or by the mistakes or malice of others, by poverty, illness or age. The people who are uneasy, not entirely comfortable at Jesus' parties, are, Jesus said, the rich, the powerful, the successful, the prestigious, the healthy, the wealthy and the well-educated. It is not that they are not invited, on the contrary, all are invited. It is just that they will often have better things to do with their lives and a better class of company to keep, and they are often otherwise engaged. Moreover, the story reflects Jesus' own experience, does it not? He had a low success-rate, or at least a mixed one, with the rich whereas the poor and the sick followed him in droves.

Now all this is truly to 'turn the world upside down'. For what Jesus called 'the world' is an attitude, one which, when we are honest, we may be able to detect ourselves sometimes sharing. The world puts at the centre of its picture of 'who belongs' to it, those who win, those who are handsome, lissom, powerful, articulate, clever, witty, photogenic, fit and usually male: a sort of Brad Pitt ideal. Like a light shed by a light bulb, it dwindles as you move closer to the periphery of its glow, so that at the edge you get the doubtful cases, people we are not so sure about as truly belonging to us: the hopelessly and haplessly poor, the demented, the comatose, the foetus, the embryo, the persistently vegetative. They, at the extreme of distance from what the world imagines to be its centre, are the people we are least sure about naming with the name we give ourselves; and so, they are the ones 'the world' is least inhibited about killing.

Jesus, I said, turns this world upside down. At the centre of his picture lie all those at the periphery of the world's picture. And it is this picture of 'who belongs' which Jesus tried to teach us by his parables. The Church ought to be, and permanently retains the instinct to try to be, the attempt to recreate this image and present it to the world, as a scandal and a shock to its system. It is this picture which informs a Christian morality in respect of the defenceless, the ill and the dying. Where the world doubts the humanity of the foetus, the Church puts it at the centre of its image; where the irreversibly dying person seems most tenuous in his hold on humanity, the Church sees a priceless moment of life. The Church does this because the Church fixes its gaze upon the image of a dying man as upon its own truth, a man executed in failure and disgrace, whom the world finds too horrible to behold and, as Isaiah says (53.5), men must turn their faces away from him in shame and disgust.

This, I think, is the true sense in which the Church is, and must be, 'pro-life'. Not that the Catholic need feel under any obligation neurotically to extend life without point, simply because we have the technology to do so. What the Church values is not the meaningless extension of years, but the dignity of death. Well, you might say, should not the Church permit the taking of life when the course of an illness robs dying of all dignity, as sometimes it does? Cannot killing ever be a mercy? The Church says no, it cannot. And the reasons lie not so much in the pragmatic doubts all may entertain about the dangers of slippery moral slopes, or in alarmist images of Nazi eugenics, good as those reasons seem to me to be. No, the heart of the matter lies hidden in the mystery of the Church, that mystery which Jesus tried to reveal to us through those parables we have been thinking about: the mystery of 'who belongs': of who belongs to us, of to whom do we most truly belong. In the end, the question all must face and to which the Church and the world give opposed answers is this: which among us most brilliantly reveals our humanity to us? Is it the powerful who know only how to take and in the end will seek to affirm their power in a last, desperate act of taking even their own lives? Or is it those who know that life is the one thing you cannot 'take', whatever you do, but may only be surrendered, returned to him by whom it was given. 'For those who possess their lives will lose them. And those who lose their lives for my name's sake, will gain them' (Matthew 16.25 and parallels).

So that is what I said to them. Now you will have to admit that this was an admirable compromise. I had been as pro-life and conservative as any right-wing Republican Catholic could have wanted, but I had chosen as grounds on which to make the case arguments which, I hoped, would challenge the position of wealth, power and status from which they themselves defended pro-life positions. I had politely complimented their food and hospitality by tying it in with the most basic instinct of the Christian, that of finding their solidarities with each other and with Christ in the breaking of bread; but I had, I thought, given sufficient notice of how that solidarity was betrayed in so far as, like their club, it excluded the poor and oppressed of the world: breaking bread sacramentally, while the poor starve for the lack of it physically, sounds not a little like 'eating and drinking judgement on yourselves', does it not? In fact I was rather pleased with myself that I had found a way of preaching to the rich uncomfortable truths without so alienating them that they would see no reason to listen at all.

But had I? I still do not know. They did not seem very disconcerted or uncomfortable. They were every bit as friendly after as before, they were flatteringly complimentary about my talk – though experience tells you to discount such comments entirely; being asked again is the only compliment that means anything, and there was in any case no question of that. I did have the impression that they rather liked the accent (which they call, quaintly, 'British'); but also that they had placed me quickly enough as a 'lefty' whose talk was as salutary as a brief penance: good for the soul, but over quickly.

I still do not know, and now do not much care whether I had achieved anything. But there is another, more general thing that I do not know, a thing which is not tested by my feeble efforts to bring it off: 'Is it possible to preach the gospel to the rich and powerful of the world?' I am not sure if even Jesus knew what the answer to this was. For sure he tried, and, as I said in my talk, he evidently had the greatest difficulty getting anywhere. Well, in any case, I do not know.

7

We Fail of Unity . . .

This slight sermon, and the next more substantial one, were preached in Church Unity Week, the first in my own parish church of Our Lady and St Rose of Lima in Weoley Castle, Birmingham in January 1998, the second in the Anglican church of Little St Mary, Cambridge, two years later. Both were composed with the same two thoughts in mind: first, our disunity is a scandal because it is an injustice to the poor; second, we have achieved very little by way of church unity, indeed, we have achieved nothing at all by way of church unity. What unity among Christians has been achieved, has been achieved by and in Christ and has been given to us already. It is for us to discover it where it is made, which is principally in our common prayer for it.

Years after Jesus died, his beloved disciple John put together a written account of all the things he remembered Jesus having said and done. We call it his 'Gospel', his telling of the good news of our salvation. You must imagine that, for many years before that, perhaps as many as sixty, John had spoken, day in and day out, to his own following within the Church; and that as he did so he would have explained the same things that he wrote about later, and perhaps many others besides, answering his disciples' questions, clarifying their difficulties, explaining one of Jesus' sayings in relation to others. And perhaps as he spoke to them, John was not too concerned to explain Jesus' words in the actual order in which Jesus had preached, but often put many sayings together in discourses to suit the purposes of his own preaching, as preachers will often do today. It is even possible that John was able to tell his own Christian disciples of many things that Jesus had said to him alone, and not to others, personally and privately in the intimacy of their friendship, so very close as that friendship was. For very close friends will say much to one another that they would not say to others.

So, when John came to write down his Gospel for his disciples, what he wrote reflected a lifetime of teaching, preaching and

explaining: and his Gospel flows from that long practice of instruct-
ing the Christian communities which gathered around him. It would
not be surprising if what he said to them reflected in some way the
concerns of a pastor, who wished to answer to the problems of his
Christian brothers and sisters, to encourage their achievements, but
also to rebuke their failures, as followers of the Master.

Sometimes, as you read John telling the story of Jesus you can
almost hear him speaking, an old man, perhaps a tired man, without
the time and energy left to be complex and sophisticated, but a man
whose long life of constant preaching, of constant prayer and of
constant recall of his Master's life has brought the words of Jesus
to a point of final profundity and complete simplicity: 'My little
children', he would say, over and over again, 'love one another.'
That, you can hear him say, is all you need to know; though Jesus
said and did enough, as John says at the end of his Gospel, 'to fill all
the books in the world', none of it means anything if it does not
mean that in word and in deed we should love one another. For 'it is
by this that you will be known as my disciples'.

If his Gospel is, as it were, John's last will and testament to his
disciples, in this too he was but following the example of his Master.
For in his telling of the events of the last supper, John puts together,
in one long final discourse, all the most profound and moving words
of Jesus that he, John, could recall – Jesus' final words to his
disciples before his death. Do you notice that those words of Jesus
are set between two startlingly opposed events, one an act of humility and love – Jesus' washing of his disciples' feet – the other an act
of pride and refusal – Judas' conspiracy to betray that love to the
'powers of the world'? And what are those words of Jesus, which are
his last will and testament to us? They are a prayer to his Father, a
prayer in every sense of the word of passion, almost a pleading, a
prayer which one might almost say is the more passionate because it
is shadowed by a doubt that it would be answered: Jesus, at the end,
prayed 'that they may be one, even as you, Father, are in me and I in
you, that they may also be in us, so that the world may believe that
you have sent me . . . that they may be one even as we are one'.

And as we sense Jesus' concern for this unity of his disciples in
service, love and humility, so we can sense the importance to John of
proclaiming to his disciples, therefore to us too, that same urgency,
that same passionate anxiety for unity. For we know that what Jesus
seemed to foresee, John had witnessed as sad fact, the disunity, the

dividedness, the rivalries and jealousies and betrayals of his disciples in his own time.

And as today, here in the Catholic Church of Our Lady and St Rose of Lima, we from many Christian traditions come together to reflect upon, to repent of and to pray with that same urgency of Jesus for the healing of our present dividedness, these thoughts are both consolation and challenge. They are a consolation of a sort, for we should not imagine that our failures of unity today are unique: they have, in different ways from our own, afflicted the Church from the very beginning, so that from its very birth in the death of its founder, the shadow of disunity and betrayal has been laid over the Church. But it is for us today a very special challenge too, because in our time at the end of the second millennium is concentrated all the accumulated dividedness of two thousand years of history: between Christians and our older brothers and sisters in Abraham, the Jews, whose religion was Jesus' own; between the Orthodox of the East and our own traditions of the West; and between us too here, divided between our Catholic traditions and those of the Churches of the great Reform of the sixteenth century; and within each of these, between rich and poor, powerful and weak; these are the dark shadows of betrayal which still hang over our prayers and our work for unity. They are a challenge, because though they are ancient history, they have gathered together and have concentrated in our time, they remain with us as living failure and as a present betrayal of witness.

Therefore, if we wish to know why it is that the world is unconvinced by us and does not know us as his disciples, will it be because our liturgy is quaint, or our theology stilted and unintelligible, or our preaching unavailable on the Internet, or because we need 'spin doctors'; or will it not rather be for the reason that Jesus himself gave us, that we are not one, that we do not love one another as Jesus has loved us?

Our path to unity is strewn with the obstacles of our small mindedness, with our petty attachments to place or language or habit of prayer and worship, with the irritations even of division and misunderstanding within our best efforts to achieve unity: for is it not true, scandalously, that when Anglicans speak to Methodists they may sometimes speak in terms they would scrupulously avoid when they speak to Catholics; or when Catholics speak to Orthodox they will skirt issues central to their dialogue with Evangelical Anglicans?

Truly our disunity is a scandal, our desire for unity enfeebled by scruple and cowardice, our prayer for unity unmoved by that urgency of passion which fired the prayer of Jesus and John.

And yet in so many ways we can, and perhaps in just enough do, wash each other's feet in service, in love and humility; enough, perhaps to offer a witness to the world, that it may believe in the Father's love of Jesus. We need not, ultimately, fear the betrayal of that witness, even our own betrayals of it, if only we will believe in the victory of love. For we have on our side a Great Advocate, the Holy Spirit, who breathes in us, if only we will let him breathe where he will and do not attempt to bind him in to us alone as our own exclusive possession, whether as individuals or as Churches. It is that same Spirit who prays in us the prayer of unity, a prayer which makes us cry out 'Abba, Father', in whom alone we are one, as Jesus was one in him and he in Jesus, making us all, in Christ, the children of God.

8

. . . But the Church is Already One

It is said nowadays that ecumenism has gone stale on us; or that it has run into the buffers (which is an apt, if not a very kind way of describing certain officials in the Vatican's Congregation for the Doctrine of the Faith); or even that it has gone into reverse, over the ordination of women, or on the issue of who counts as a 'sister Church'. And I think that this pessimism is unwarranted, though if there are reasons for discouragement they would rather lie in the fact that even the successes, say of the Anglican–Roman Catholic International Commission (ARCIC) – some of ARCIC's agreed theological documents are successes – have achieved so little else than to satisfy the committees which compiled them. And if, in turn, there is a reason for that, it might be that too much official ecumenical activity between our two Churches has looked like piecemeal negotiation, is too fragmentary, too preoccupied with the identification of agreed, neutralizing, forms of words, agreed words which are still too fearful of the divisive power and vibrancy of each other's dialects. It was said, often enough, that those documents did their theology as it were in a dialect no practising Christian spoke: Geordies and Cockneys as we were, for the purposes of doing theology ecumenically, we agreed for the nonce to speak Essex, or West Country, or, God help us, Brummie – or perhaps, the better analogy is with what used to be called 'received pronunciation', which I gather no one, not even the Queen, speaks any more.

One way or another, the problems which the ecumenical project encounters nowadays seem often to derive from its still being thought of as something additional. Additional, that is to our given churchmanship; additional to the theological enterprise which we might undertake, if we are theologians, within and for our own faith communities. And this is as true of the ecumenical optimists as it is of the pessimists.

It is true of those optimists, who suppose that ecclesial boundaries and historical identities do not matter at all, and so, for example imagine that there really isn't a problem about intercommunion except for the hidebound: but they leave denominationally loyal Christians in the lurch, with nowhere to go.

And it is true of those pessimists who appear to think that boundaries and identities matter more than anything else could, though perhaps if essentials are not compromised, an annual trip to the local Baptist church in January can probably do no harm.

Both optimists and pessimists speak from nowhere to no one and either marginalize ecumenism as the province of the specialists or else marginalize the Churches as the last resort of the sectarians. Both add little except to reinforce a sense of the alienated and alienating character of the ecumenical project.

And I don't suppose that this is a theological problem only. For which of us, after all, is there not some inclination, if only a residual one, but one which nonetheless is capable of being elicited from time to time with the character of lively feeling, that the real thing is to be found in what we do each in separation, that the things we do together have a certain additional, supernumerary character?

Well, perhaps I ought only to speak for myself. So I shall. I am a Roman Catholic. I grew up a Roman Catholic as a teenager in the 1950s believing that our English Catholic history was marked by three centuries of persecution and hostility to, and a fourth century of marginalization of, my beliefs about the real presence of Christ in the Eucharist. So it is not surprising that I knew what the Roman Catholic Bishops of England and Wales meant when they insisted, in a document called *One Bread, One Body*, that English Catholics tie their identity in very closely with a sense of – well, as I should say, though not the Bishops – near exclusive possessiveness about the Blessed Sacrament of the altar: that, we feel, is *our* thing.

Well, of course I know better than to think that, much better than to say it: nonetheless, as people who do a lot of thinking know better than most, thinking is a poor remedy for temptations and much thinking the poorest of all. In any case, my temptations are otherwise than what I know I should properly think: I still find, even in a singularly un-Protestant church of the Anglican Communion, that I am assailed by an instinct that there is something missing here that I would feel at home with in the church of Our Lady and the English Martyrs. I imagine a Protestant being similarly assailed in my church, or in Little St Mary's, when I, and perhaps you, bless ourselves with holy water and genuflect to the Blessed Sacrament. And for your part, have you not winced at the Vatican's document *Dominus Iesus* which recently declared yours not to be a 'sister Church' and thus declared your temptations? The trouble for me is that I have winced at *Dominus Iesus* too – about as much as I wince sometimes at the establishment of the Church of England. Temptations are often thus complex. They may not add up: but they are not the less powerful for all that.

Our first reading (Exodus 24) reminded us that the assembly possesses one law, which it can read with confidence as its common language: and don't we all weep for much the same reasons? Our second reading (Acts 2) is important because it reminds us that, though in possession of a common language, we speak many dialects; that we understand one another because we listen to each other's dialects, not because we have abandoned our native accents for some neutral tongue which none of us possess, but because our commonality lies in the attentiveness of our listening.

Now I know that, as to that law read before the assembly, it is commonly said that God revealed it to that people. But it might equally be said that that law is what revealed God to them, for it made the people of Israel to be a people by giving them the justice they were to live by. Israel's God was shown forth in and through the justice in which was rooted their common identity. Exodus tells us, the people of Israel will know their God in and through the justice which they will do to one another, so that the failure to do that justice is – not that it will have the consequence of, but is – idolatry. And the gospel reading (Luke 4) completes the exegesis: the assembly will reveal the true God in that justice which brings good news to the poor.

There are those who have derived from this Lucan passage some general conclusions about what gets called, inelegantly – alas, how very inelegant is so much theological writing – the 'priority of praxis over theory', in orthopraxis rather than orthodoxy; which would appear to mean that ecumenism would be better served if we were to forget about the merely 'internal', ecclesial and doctrinal issues of intercommunion, or ministry, or apostolicity, or whatever, and give priority to the common active ministry of social justice. It seems to be suggested that those other ecclesial issues will by such means sort themselves out in consequence.

I doubt if this is wise advice. Ecclesial issues of unity are never 'mere'. In any case, I do not think Christians can know what they have distinctively to say about justice in the wider community, until they can witness it as the reality which constitutes their own assemblies. And for sure that is the implication which the conjunction of our readings today presses upon us: it is our unity alone which can bind together the bringing of good news to the poor with the proclamation of the one true God's mercy and love, so that neither is prior to the other, our condition of unity as a Church and our practice of justice in the world. We can do that justice to the poor which reveals God only if we are truly the assembly which speaks, in so many dialects, of one justice, and knows its God in and through its unity.

But if that is so, then our disunity is at once a kind of idolatry and a kind of failure of justice: not, I repeat, that it has that consequence, but that it is idolatrous. The disunities we visit upon one another we inevitably visit on everyone else; and the extent of our double failure of unity and solidarity is the extent to which we give false revelation of God.

But what, in fact, is the extent of our disunity – I mean, in fact, and today? How dismayed ought we to be? Well, let me here be simple-minded, for I am a simple-minded layman. Here's simple-mindedness for you: Jesus was able to predict, because he could guarantee it, that 'the gates of hell will not prevail against [this Church]' (Matthew 16.18). I think it absolutely essential that we remain firm in that truth: in spite of depressing evidence to the contrary, the Church is already one, as it is already holy, catholic and apostolic. It is those things, or else the mission of Christ has already failed.

So long as, but only if, we are utterly steadfast in that truth can we look with unmitigated realism at the patent facts of our disunities and not be aghast at them as ultimate scandal. Being penultimately scandalous they define the agenda, as also the urgency, of our present ecumenical task: being only penultimately scandalous, they cannot be its ultimate failure. Perhaps we Christians are more one than we know, more hurt by our differences than we have need to be; perhaps the search for our unity is less the recreation of something lost so much as the search for something which is already there and always has been, but misrecognized.

Quaesivi, et non inveni, 'I searched, and I did not find him', the bride in the Song of Songs (3.1, 2) cries. Perhaps even the great historical events of our schism were, if of course scandalous, also mysteriously necessary if the story of the unity which Christ promised to us is to be adequately told. Perhaps. What is certain is that our unity is a great gift, and that we already possess it and always will: but it is also a great mystery, so it is not surprising if we are always at a loss to comprehend it and cannot see it for where it is.

It is also for this reason that we should not be too confident of knowing what the 'goal of final visible unity', as it is sometimes called, would look like if we were to achieve it.

In one sense, we already possess it, even if, like partners in a marriage in crisis, we are often both missing the point, both looking in the wrong direction for it, failing to see the depths of our true unity where they are to be found. So even when it is given to us to take for free, we are still very likely to misrecognize it and be disheartened, thinking it unavailable.

But also in the sense in which it remains as a present task, something still to be worked for, here too we must accept that any humanly devised construal of that unity will still fail of ultimate comprehension of that unity and peace which Jesus gave us, for it is not of this world, and the world does not know it.

So here, as today and this week, we pray for that unity, as very properly we do, we pray, as we always do when we pray together, for a *fait accompli*, and therefore with confidence. For as Thomas Aquinas wrote, it is not the case that God is caused by our prayers to will what we seek; rather it is that God infallibly wills to grant what we seek through our praying for it. So there is a certain sense in which in our praying here and now for the unity of the Church, we are both making the unity which we pray for and revealing something of its mystery as already present.

Quaesivi et non inveni: that's true, for that unity is a mystery beyond all that we could know to seek for, for, as St Paul says, we do not know how to pray as we should. But the unity we seek is also already present in the seeking itself, for it is the one Spirit who prays in us, and so it is in our prayers for unity that that unity is already achieved – because our heavenly Father has willed to grant us his kingdom through, and in, our asking for it.

Therefore, as we pray today for that unity, let us also thank our Father in heaven; confessing our failure, for sure, but not disheartened by it; therefore let us pray also with joy, because our prayers together, and especially this week, are themselves a gift of unity which our heavenly Father wills for us through them.

How to Remember

The three sermons which follow were all preached at services of commemoration, and naturally take as their theme the nature and quality of our remembering. The first was preached on Remembrance Sunday in 1996 in Birmingham's Anglican Cathedral; the second, at a service celebrating the twentieth anniversary in 1997 of St Mary's Hospice in Selly Park, Birmingham, of which I was for a short time a trustee; the third, in 2001 at Peterhouse, my college at Cambridge, on the occasion of the annual service of Commemoration of Benefactors. How we remember matters, whether with honesty or with self-deception, for how and what we remember makes us what we are, makes our identities. But how we are to remember with hope remains a problem when honesty has us recall from our pasts, whether personal or institutional, much we would recoil from celebrating.

9

Remembering War

I once described to my mother an event of my early childhood and, rather pleased with my powers of recall, I gave her a quite detailed account. When I had finished, she smiled, and said simply: 'You are exactly right in every detail, except for one thing. It wasn't you that happened to, it was your younger brother.'

Hardly a major identity crisis, you might say, even in the insignificant tabloid of my own daily record of events. And, it must be said, the event I had so misremembered was very trivial, something, as I had thought, about how I had reacted to an upset on my fifth birthday. Yet I have to confess that I was a little disconcerted. I was quite pleased with the memory. If nothing really crucial to my sense of selfhood had been threatened, still I do not have too many childhood memories and in a small way I treasured this one. It was a friendly bit of my past, and not everything in that great cavern of past events is as innocent and unthreatening as this memory had seemed to be.

Is not memory a strange and dangerous power? 'A vast storehouse' St Augustine once called it, out of which we can pick and choose at will. Yet such things it contains!

Some memories are well-loved treasures, and we are only too pleased to take them out and polish them up, admire them and place them in the front room of our living space, for they are pleasing reminders of those we have loved; and perhaps this is especially so when it is our self-esteem which is at stake, for we will gratefully give house-room to those friendly memories which flatter a kinder picture of ourselves than we think, perhaps, we truly deserve.

Some memories, on the contrary, we retrieve with pleasure but mainly to hurt others with, for they serve on mind's mantelpiece to refresh our present resentment. Other memories, many perhaps, we are only too glad to lose, because their retrieval would hurt us too much; some we hope are still there, only we are reluctant to seek them out, lest the fear be confirmed that they were never there at all.

Good memories and bad memories, the stuff of our hopes and

equally of our nightmares, we are, in our present recall of them, either liberated by or trapped within them; and we live either reconciled with our memories in honest repentance, acceptance and hope, or else out of kilter with them in the distortions of shame, guilt, resentment, self-deception and remorse; and very probably with some of both. For who can stand honestly and without shame, truthfully and without the deepest pain, before all that his storehouse contains?

Ancient Christian writers, throughout the Patristic and medieval periods, reflected much on this power of memory. So fundamental did they see this human power to be within the work of our restoration from sin, that they assigned to its redemption one of the three theological virtues: as faith is to our human power of knowing, they said, and charity is to our human power of loving, so is hope to memory. And with good reason they said this. When, in our final judgement, we stand before the blinding, searing light of God, all will be exposed, everything in that storehouse of memory will be taken out into the open; and who, in a cold and loveless light, could resist despair at the onset of so much reality? Whose rest and peace would not be disturbed by the sweating nightmare of so much self-knowledge? For which of us would so much truth not be a veritable hell? Who, without hope, without an ultimate, unconditional trust in a divine compassion, which only love can sustain, could find in that light of memory's day anything but a cold, ultimate desolation?

Here, in our half-lit world, we can stand only so much reality. Where the truth is too much for us, we suppress it or else invent an alternative. We are, in our present reality, the story we have made out of our selected memories, more or less truthful, and only more or less lovable, because, as with all our loves, so with our love of self, we are afraid to love unconditionally. Indeed, sometimes we even invent spurious theologies, or quasi-religious attitudes, as reassurance that we have no need to love ourselves beyond a certain point. And we do not love ourselves unconditionally, because we are afraid to know ourselves unconditionally; and we are afraid to know ourselves unconditionally because we doubt our capacity to like what we fear we would discover if we did. Perfect memory without love is hell. Which is why, our love being partial and compromised, we can afford at best a compromise with partial, selected, memories.

I sometimes think, blasphemously, that Jesus got just one thing wrong from the point of view of our twentieth-century predicament:

for he told us that we should love our neighbour as ourselves. I wonder though if it would not be better were we to love ourselves with a little more of the ease with which we love our neighbours: or at least if we remembered that God can love us only unconditionally; that is to say, he can love only the whole truth of us, the ugliness and the beauty, and it is that truth of our ambiguity, not our supposed worthiness, which seduces him: for 'it is his delight to play with the sons of men'. On the contrary, he is repelled only by our attempts to refashion a false and, as we think of it, a more lovable, a more worthy, fiction.

Shortly, we will perform together that ultimately redeeming act of remembering which signifies and effects our unity as Christians. It is a unity signified and made real in our daily memory of a cruel miscarriage of justice, the judicial execution not merely, as we put it in an anodyne phrase, of an 'innocent man', but of a man who loved with that intensity of unconditional love that is of God alone, indeed is God. And that death was not merely caused by our sin, it reveals sin for what it is: the need we have to refuse unconditional love. So we killed him. The death of that man, conveniently executed 'for the sake of the people', represents the short-term victory of an ultimate 'short-termism'; the victory of a love compromised by utility over a love utterly unconditional.

I stand today in a church of the Anglican communion, a Church whose complex relations with the people of our nation I confess, as a Roman Catholic, I do not always understand; but today at least I do. For today our nation remembers events of our times as full of cruelty, destruction, barbarism and violence as it is possible for human beings to engage in: war. And if our Church must take its share of the nation's responsibility for remembering these things, may it do so worthily if it is not filled with a profound sense of the difficulty, indeed of the impossibility, of doing so with adequacy? How may the Church remember war with any integrity in the name of Christ, if it does so neglectful of its own foundation in an act of infinitely compassionate reconciliation and forgiveness? For the Church has no other foundation.

You will not ask me to spell out the details of what we are challenged to remember today: I shall say only one thing about this. You do not remember with Christian adequacy the wars of our nation in the twentieth century if you think that the morality of doing so is unproblematic. For war is evil. If war is ever justified, it is still evil.

If all the wars we have fought as a nation in this century have been necessary to prevent greater evils, they have still been evils. Today, then, we drag up some dreadful evils from our past and place them before our eyes: and we must, if we are to be faithful to our calling as Christians, learn again how to do so with truth and realism, how to stare those realities fully in the face, without flinching; but we will be able to do so only in that faith, hope and love which will enable us to remember the reality of those wars with truthfulness. For though the past is the past, our memory of it is part of our present reality as a nation: and casually or wilfully to misremember that past is to live a present lie.

In this century, then, we have sent millions of our young people abroad, on land and sea and in the air, and to do what? I am afraid that the truth of the matter is that we sent them abroad to kill other young people, of other nations. We sent them abroad and we, and they, perhaps in the vast majority, did so their consciences satisfied that what they were sent to do was, if appalling, nonetheless necessary: and so an appalling necessity. I know that not every Christian, then or now, could reconcile the horror of that mission with their consciences, and I do not think it wise on this occasion to rehearse those conflicts of conscience. But if we are not, by our present memories, to betray those people who died in our defence, then in honesty we must reflect on the horrendous responsibility we undertake in justifying what we and they did.

Imagine that members of your family, or close friends, were to find themselves in the situation that they could defend your life and that of the rest of your family, and all the values you treasure, only if they killed, deliberately and with intent, some other people; suppose that thereby they ran the equal risk that they would themselves be killed in the attempt; and suppose that they would do it only on the condition of your consent. How easy would you find it in your conscience to give that consent? And suppose you gave it and you and your family were saved, except that, as a result of your agreeing to the deal, some of them were killed too. Just how would it be right to mark the anniversary of those events? In what frame of mind would it be right to remember them? How do you consent to a man's killing in your name, for your safety and security? Are we not humiliated by the responsibility we have assumed so many times in this century? What burdens of conscience we have carried and required others to carry; and how lightly do we remember what was done in our name if we fail to remember that responsibility, when we remember the heroism and self-sacrifice of those who carried those burdens for us. For do we not trivialize the heroism, the self-sacrifice, the comradeship and the solidarities that the wars of our times undoubtedly occasioned, if we rob those wars of their similar, but immensely intensified, moral ambiguities?

And how are we to remember those of hostile nations whom our young people killed, many of whom, in turn, no doubt killed some of our own? And some did much worse. Can we forgive them? In our times of cheap moralizing, this seems to be an issue. Some say yes, all acts, all people, must be forgiven; some say no, some people, some acts are unforgivable. For my part, I merely ask, whence is our power to forgive any person, any act? In the Lord's Prayer, we pray that we will be forgiven as we forgive, and one hears it said that in praying thus we ask that God will forgive us only on the condition and to the extent that we forgive each other. True hostages to fortune that would be! God help us if Jesus intended a bargain as hard as that! Or rather, if he had, would it not mean that not even God will help us if we fail in our forgiveness. And which of us does not know that of all the things for which we need an infinite forgiveness, it is for our failure to forgive that we need it?

I find it wholly satisfying to the fraught and incomprehensible difficulty of this remembering, that that burned cross of wood, constructed out of the fragments of the ruined Cathedral in Coventry, has written upon it the simple words: 'Father forgive'. 'Father forgive', it says, not 'We forgive', for we have no power to forgive if it is not because the Father has forgiven us first. Nor, you will note, 'Father forgive them', as if the only ones who needed that forgiveness were our enemies who did it; not 'for they know not what they do', for if not those combatants themselves, then at least their superiors, knew very well what they did. But simply, and universally and without exception made of anyone: 'Father forgive'.

For that, in the end, is all that it is possible for memory to say. War is a horrible reality. But it is also a stark metaphor of all the accumulated evil that is in the world, that mass of evil in which are interwoven, inseparably, elements of our own personal responsibility – for it is our acts and our own complicities which make wars – together with impersonal, implacable powers of evil which are beyond our capacity to control, or even make any sense of. There is the evil, then, that we do, our sins, and we can make a certain sense of them through our freedom and the seductions of its misuse; but there is the evil which we are in, bigger, more powerful than we are, overwhelming us with its utter senselessness; and in a theologically more self-confident age, we called it the sin which was 'original', visited upon us, implicating us with a collective responsibility from which there is no unravelling of our own, personal, responsibility.

Before the reality of that evil we have no power of our own except to utter a helpless plea: 'Father forgive'. It is a prayer which Jesus uttered for us, for unless he did we would be helpless even to utter it on our own behalf. And he did so on the cross, dying a barbaric and senseless death, with our consent: and as we remember our wars and all those who killed and died in them, let us do so in the only way which contains the certainty of a memory redeemed: doing that thing which shortly we will do, as he asked us, 'in memory of me'.

10

Remembering the Dying

'Actions speak louder than words', they say; but when you think about it, this truism doesn't tell us that actions are necessarily more important than words, but that when it comes to the business of communicating messages, to the business of 'speaking', it is often actions which speak the more effectively, at times and places where words alone are inadequate and fail us.

You won't mind me being very briefly philosophical about this. Every single thing in our world 'acts' in some way. It is one of the miracles of physics in the twentieth century to have discovered just how busily active even the smallest particles of matter we can identify are: within neutrons there are whole worlds of frenzied activity, multiple forms of energy. One hundred years ago we thought matter was a structure of inert, passive lumps. Now we know that matter is a railway station at rush hour. And at the other end of the scale of magnitudes, astronomers astonish us with tales of energies in deep space so vast and intense that they can imprison even light itself in 'black holes'. And if even dead matter, in all our previous cultures the very symbol of passivity and inertness, turns out for us in the late twentieth century to be made of energies and actions, how much the more so will the world of living organisms, whose very notion is that of 'action', be a field of doing and making and unmaking and organizing and directing and constructing and deconstructing?

So you might say that 'action' is the ordinary stuff of our universe; everything is at it all the time, and the cessation of activity is death. But speaking is not ordinary. Only some beings do it. And we human beings seem to be the only creatures whose actions are capable of speaking, as we say, 'louder than words': as they do when we silently hug a grieving friend, send flowers to an absent lover, or give an uncalled-for smile to a passing stranger.

I say this, because we could be distracted into celebrating twenty years of St Mary's Hospice mainly by recording the intense activity of those years: the inspired labour of origins, the endless rounds of meetings – no doubt many of them tedious and wastefully long – the

fundraising, the negotiating, the planning, the building, the inter-
viewing, the employing, the caring, the administrating of an ever
more complex organization – all those things which have occupied
and preoccupied so many people, who have given time and money
and energy to the visible, palpable success of St Mary's Hospice
today, twenty years on. It is right that we should use this occasion as
an opportunity for thanksgiving for all that.

But we do not thank all those countless people well, nor honour
the sacrifice of their activity, if we forget what all that doing says, the
story it tells. For we are here today standing not just for ourselves
but also for all those people over twenty years who have given of
themselves, often in the face of great difficulties and obstacles, in
ways which I am sure will have sometimes seemed unrewarded; but
they have done all this in this place, St Mary's, because of something
very special which they thought their actions could and would say.
And I think that what St Mary's has to say is something very special,
something very fundamental, something more often than not
missed, about what it is to be human.

For St Mary's is a place where we have gathered together, deliberately, of set purpose, openly, publicly – in fulfilment of what we
call our mission – to declare the absolutely central fact about what
it is to be human: that we decay, that we suffer, and that we die: in
short, that we humans fail. We, here, organize ourselves around this
fact of human failure, though what I call a 'fact' of human failure
should more properly be regarded as the 'mystery' of human failure.
I am tempted to say that St Mary's is human failure made into a sort
of sacrament.

And it is for this reason that we should today consider why it is
that actions speak louder than words. For here in St Mary's we have
put at the centre of our work human realities of suffering and death
before which words have failed, human situations of suffering and
pain and tragedy before which none of us knows what to say which
has any adequacy to the case. Which is natural enough: for in our
health, we think of death more or less as a distant horizon, an edge,
as it were, to our day-to-day experience of living. We do not often
have reason to look at the horizon itself until we are struck down by
illness, or the death of someone close, or by other tragedy. Here
though, we foreground the horizon, the edge moves to the centre,
and we are disabled in our ordinary human capacities for explanation, our workaday, practical reasons for things lose relevance and

point. In that sense, all of us here, carers and patients, are equally confronted by our common human predicament, equally confounded, equally lost for words.

Which is why we allow our actions to speak, to say those things which our words cannot. Which is why we do not preach, we do not moralize. We are intensely practical. But we know where we stand. We are repelled by jargonized evasions of the cruel realities of our human condition. But we find equally repugnant those false spiritualities which make an idol out of unnecessary pain and discomfort. We do not technologize death away, depriving it of all significance except as medical failure. But we actively fund research into more adequate methods of terminal care. And if we do not preach we do wish to share our experience with others, we do wish to educate, to join with the medical professions in the training of carers. But we do all of this out of a deep conviction which is, as it were, the silent speech lying within our actions; and that silent speech says that the loneliness of suffering and the remorseless inevitability of death need not, for us human beings, be nothing but separation and departure, but on the contrary, can be a gateway into a profound human solidarity, an entry into a discovery which is not possible for us by any other means. For we are human beings, and for us there just is no other way, 'That's life', you might say. Just so. That is why we can say, and must always say, that what we are about is not death and dying, but about life and living.

It is true to say that we do not force even this common, very human, meaning on anyone. For we possess no monopoly on any means or meanings. We simply try to make it available to everyone, allowing each patient, in their faith of whatever kind, or in their rejection of faith, to take from us what we have to give: and even if they take nothing in the end, we still give it, because what we have created here is, in the last resort, a place for the exchange of gifts, a place in which we give each other the gift of our humanity and so learn from each other that primitive, ultimate fact which governs all our understanding of what death and dying are: that our humanity is essentially gift, not something we have won and own by right of disposal, but is something given to us and given by us each to one another.

And we, some of us, find in all this a deeper significance of faith and in that human depth find a divine significance, an utterance of a divine love at once completely beyond our words and our comprehension and at the same time almost unbearably intimate and close. But here too, perhaps more particularly here, we do not, as I say, insist upon that significance of faith, still less on any particular traditions of it, as if that knowledge too were some privileged possession of our own, at our disposal to deliver in neat packages of meaning and sense to a senseless world. For faith does not clear up the mysteries of death and dying; it only deepens them. But it does give those mysteries a name, for they are mysteries of love and messages of its victory. Some will share that name with us, others will not: but that love which sustains our giving and receiving from one another needs no name to be present in our giving and receiving, for you can enjoy the song without knowing the name of the singer and in ignorance of who composed it.

Today, then, we celebrate twenty years of witness, of words spoken by countless deeds which have silently spoken of these and many other things. And we have much to be thankful for, still more to do and upon us lies more obligation than ever to be saying what St Mary's says, doing what we do. For ours is a world which seems less able than twenty years ago, not more, to offer a reason, a foundation, an understanding of life within which to contemplate and live death as life. In a vast, complex, powerful world, we are but a little, fairly powerless thing, a 'still small voice of calm' in a clamour of denial and refusal. But in what we failingly and inadequately strive to do and to be, act and represent, we say something which that world needs to hear, even if often it would rather not listen.

11

Remembering Benefactors

We commemorate our benefactors in Peterhouse today by means of divine worship and a feast. And it is worthwhile reminding the puritans – supposing any to have penetrated our usually secure defences – that if there is to be any true association between these two forms of celebration, divine worship and eating, as, in the Christian and other traditions there very properly is, then not only the worship, but also the food, needs to be worthy of a feast. No doubt, shortly, it will be. Herbert McCabe, the Dominican theologian, was once asked by some liberal-minded young person, why it was that in their eucharistic celebrations Christians persisted with the consecration of the archaic materials of bread and wine, rather than of something more up-to-date and relevant, like hot dogs and coke. To which Herbert replied that he had always supposed the Eucharist to have something to do with the meaning of food, and hot-dogs and coke are without meaning and anyway are not food. Just so. And although this evening our worship is not of the eucharistic variety, nonetheless the association remains: we worship and we feast and perhaps should feel no shame if we confuse the two, for the worship shades into the feast and the feast into the worship. There could, however, be no possibility of so excellent a theological confusion in a McDonald's.

On the other hand, there did occur a momentary scruple, conceivably of a puritanical sort, when I contemplated the benefactors whom we are commemorating today, the list of which the Dean has just read. Ought I to research them, as others in the past seem to have done when discharging this responsibility? Or, in view of what one might turn up about the personal credentials of some of them, might it be better not to know too much? That list is a sort of Peterhouse genealogy, readily calling to mind another even more famous genealogy, found at the beginning of Matthew's Gospel, which tells of the ancestry of Jesus Christ. Matthew's genealogy is a consolation to a preacher at today's feast, for Peterhouse could hardly have worse fortune on the score of ancestors than Jesus did, seeing that his forebears were on the whole a thoroughly disreputable lot. Matthew counts among them but few worthies, and otherwise an assortment of rapists, torturers, adulterers, murderers, robbers, prostitutes and traitors. Which only goes to show that you don't have to have a good pedigree to turn out all right in the end.

Which is why I suppose we can with good conscience celebrate and commemorate our benefactors without having to concoct some cock-and-bull story about the degree of their moral probity. As I say, I did not attempt to research our benefactors' moral credentials, and I therefore have no reason in fact to doubt their excellence. But I do know, brief as has been my acquaintance with Peterhouse, that on another occasion we manage to do justice to our former Master, Mr Perne, with a note on our menu card which does not neglect to note that he possessed, let us say, a certain plasticity of conscience. So I know that this service is a formal and ritual affair of thanksgiving to them, but formal and ritual as it may be, there is no reason, on that account, why it should lack all honesty and historical accuracy. For there is a danger of a commemoration which is at once exaggerated in piety and vacuous, as if we, now, need the reassurance of a past which exceeds morally any reasonable standard we would aspire to today. Peterhouse is, no doubt, ordinarily imperfect now. It does not need to represent itself as having been perfect then.

I say these things, you might think inappropriately, but because, I suppose, this day has the significance for us that we remind ourselves, as it were, of the importance of memory; that is to say, we not only remember, we also celebrate the remembering itself, as a present act, making it so important in our collective lives as a college, that we go to the trouble of formally marking its importance by making an annual meal of it. And with good reason: for, as the ancient Christian Fathers used to know, memory in a person is the seat of identity; and as with persons, so with institutions; and perhaps especially with communities of scholars, who, being the highly-strung, individualistic characters that we commonly are, are not easily got to congregate around collective identities. We especially need to remember with accuracy and honesty, for to us what will matter more than to most is the quality of the remembering itself. And the trouble with that academic obsession with accuracy and honesty, is that the rather mixed moral quality of the ancestry can too easily draw honest memory into a cynicism corrosive of our collective identity; and then inhibiting of our capacity to celebrate. It is hard to construct defences completely secure against the puritans, or, which is to say the same, against the cynics.

So how may we do it? That is, how may we at once remember our benefactors with the honesty of scholars, and at the same time with ritual adequacy give expression to a gratitude which, as it were, gathers together that accumulated, morally mixed history of benefaction within a present celebratory act? We owe our present opportunity to those men and women who endowed us: for certain some did it (I would by no means deny it) out of pure generosity of spirit; perhaps some endowed us out of a purer conviction than we ourselves can manage, of the scholarly values which we espouse; perhaps in some cases they gave out of bad conscience; perhaps even, in a few worst cases, they gave to buy a temporal privilege they could not earn on merit; and for sure, in earliest times, some gave to buy an eternal privilege they doubted their chances of gaining by other means. Yet today we commemorate them all, the cynical place-seekers, the morally ambiguous, and the selflessly generous, equally and without distinction.

And so we should. For those ancient Christian writers, who saw memory as the seat of identity, did so only in so far as memory constructed and contained, as present act, not only an honest, undeceived narrative of the past, but also those opportunities for the future which are released by hope. Memory without hope is cynicism and denies the future. Well, then, the cynic's clarity sees all, but at no antecedent cost. The price he eventually pays is, however, ultimate, and comes in the payback as consequence; for in the lucidity of his gaze the cynic sees through everything and therefore sees nothing. For the cynic, everything lacks density, ground, substance. Including, in the end, himself.

On the other hand, hope without honest memory is groundless optimism. For the optimist there is only a vacuous and feckless immediacy: in lacking a past, the optimist, like the cynic, also lacks future. Both the cynic and the optimist lack hope because in one way or another they destroy the past. Hence, neither can properly celebrate because for the cynic, memory comes in the form only of resentment; for the optimist, memory is suppressed out of fear that the cynic is all too likely to be right.

And so neither can live with any degree of comfort with the reality of time; with time, that is to say, in which alone narrative, history, and therefore identity, can breathe freely the air of past, present and future, without regret, without succumbing to the tyranny of any one of these over the other. Not to the tyranny of the past which permits of no further possibilities than it already contains; nor to the tyranny of the present which denies meaning and moral force equally to past and future; nor to that tyranny of the future which concedes no substance to the present moment, but only an anxiety for the next step. Only that wholeness of memory, which lives in a present in which past and future, memory and hope, conjoin and sustain one another, and make, as a Christian author of the eighteenth century put it, a 'sacrament of the present moment'; only a memory of that kind can liberate the possibility of a commemoration which is celebratory, a meal which is thanksgiving, a communion of fellows in the wholeness of time.

In such a memorial, carried out by imperfect men and women in commemoration of men and women no less imperfect, we do something which altogether transcends, and in a way redeems, the tawdry narrative of the motives of either. For in remembering our benefactors we commemorate those who made our presence here as Petreans any kind of possibility; and so our debt to them has an unconditional character, for their moral credentials and their motives are, in point of that at least, irrelevant; as also are our own. And so our pleasure in the celebration can be unconditional too, untroubled by puritan scruple.

Of which scruple you may say that it had not occurred to you to be troubled by it. But then, if not today to yield to it, might it not be a better thing at least on occasion to have entertained it, with that honesty which only hope permits, and then to celebrate with good conscience? For after all, it was those our benefactors who made that hope a possibility for us.

Prayer

How I found myself, in February 1999, conducting a 'day of recollection' for seminarians at Oscott College, the Birmingham Archdiocesan Seminary, on the subject of 'prayer', I shall never know. For I am no preacher, and shudder to think of myself in any role of spiritual guide. In any event, the two talks and short homily which follow, are more 'personal' than anything else in this collection, because although I have read many theological writings on the subject of prayer, I had never read anything which started from the low levels of good practice from which I knew I started. So I decided to speak out of my own personal experience of praying within and out of my own mental and emotional chaotic inadequacy – just in case there were any young men in the seminary who were still supposing (it was very unlikely) that there was some more mature spiritual condition they ought to be praying out of.

The other two sermons were delivered to university students, the first, on praying in the Spirit, at Sunday Mass in the Catholic Chaplaincy in the University of Birmingham; and the second, to some students and fellows (but mainly to uncomprehending tourists) at Evensong in King's College Chapel in May 2001. These two sermons set prayer where it should be set within the Church's celebration of the Eucharist. Whereas the Oscott pieces might have been called 'praying in the desert', the other two might well have been called 'praying in the body', or 'in the resurrection'. They may help to correct what might appear to be an excessive individualism in the Oscott talks.

12

How not to Pray

'We do not know how to pray as we ought' (Romans 8.26), says St Paul, and I do not think that he meant simply that we, or the Christians he was addressing, happened not to be very good at praying, though with more practice, or greater effort, they might become better at it. I think he meant that not being good at it was in the nature of prayer, and in our nature too: that given what prayer is, we could not, in the nature of things, be any good at it.

I think this ought to console us. It is particularly consoling for me, for I have chosen to speak to you today chiefly on the subject of prayer and I do so very especially conscious of inadequacy. I am no good at it; but then I have often observed among those who preach that they are at their best when speaking of those matters in which they are most conscious of failure, for they know the difficulties from the inside as it were and can speak sympathetically to the rest of us.

Also, I have the idea that I am under no obligation to tell you anything wise, or very spiritual, about prayer, for did not Jesus tell us that we are not, any of us, to call ourselves teachers of one another, for we have only one teacher, and he is our Father in heaven. All of us who have any task of teaching or instruction in the Church ought to take that very seriously, for it means that when we Christians speak to one another, as on an occasion like this, we must be sure that we have nothing to offer of our own; for we gather together here to remind each other only of what we have already been given and already share, a common gospel and a common grace; our task is to explain and remind and exhort, not to add or take away our insignificant jots and tittles.

So I begin with St Paul saying that we do not know how to pray as we ought and with that evidence of failure in prayer which is our own experience of inadequacy. I speak for myself here, and merely ask you to reflect for yourselves whether or not for you, as for me, your experience of prayer is normally the experience of failure. But then if St Paul is right, why should we mind when our attempts to pray turn out to be more than usually disastrous? And would we not be very foolishly misled if we supposed that our credentials for speaking on the subject had to lie in our degree of success in prayer when, as St Paul says, we do not know how to do it. To me, it seems that we at least know something, and something essential, about prayer if we know that we are no good at it because we *couldn't* be good at it – and that, very largely, because there isn't anything to be good at – when it comes to prayer.

I think, however, that this matters in a personal way. I do know that for my part I spent many years resisting and then resenting the fact that my attempts to pray were more or less a complete disaster; and that was how things stood until something made me realize what St Paul meant: to suppose that success in prayer was measurable by the success of my experience of it was to lie under a powerful illusion that somehow or other prayer could and should be an observably successful, obviously beneficial, personally meaningful activity – all those things I very rarely found it to be. So until you have learned to dispel that illusion what you do – perhaps, if you are exceptionally obtuse, for a long while – is to try harder and thus compound the cause of the failure – which is, of course, the very efforts you make to succeed.

As a result, you very soon find yourself resenting your failure and then, perhaps, you give up. Or perhaps you make the discovery that it is your efforts which are the problem. Perhaps you will know the words of the Angel to Gerontius in Newman's *Dream*: 'it is thy very strenuousness of thought which keeps thee from thy God'. De Caussade meant much the same, I guess, when he asked us to 'Rejoice every day when you discover a new defect.' For when it comes to prayer, weakness, and the knowledge of it, really is our only strength.

Just to be sure that we know what we are talking about here – for I take nothing for granted on the subject of how or when you pray – I am talking about what we have traditionally imagined Jesus was up to when he retired for forty days in the desert, as we hear the story told today; and I refer to the desert he advised us to find 'in your own room', there to 'pray to your Father in secret', for there 'your Father who is in secret will reward you' (Matthew 6.6), as we heard last week on Ash Wednesday. Well, I suppose we ought not to be surprised if, in the desert of our own room, we encounter much the same as Jesus did, many a temptation. Why, therefore, should you be scandalized at the thought that praying on your own like this, persevered with regularly, is on many occasions a tiresome, distracted, tedious, seemingly pointless occupation, which seems to get us nowhere, inspire us to little and to have no very obviously improving effects on our lives? How very much in secret sometimes is our heavenly Father's reward!

Of course, you won't find prayer to be like this unless you make a regular, habitual practice of it. For if you merely pray to taste, prayer will always be to your taste, but we can learn nothing from the effeteness of the gourmet who picks and chooses and ignores sound nutrition because it is dull. Prayer is less like a banquet than a good breakfast; porridge is easy to get out of the habit of, thin on uplift and good for you only if you take the trouble to get up in time to make it and then aren't too greedy for instant results.

And we are, as John of the Cross says, all too often greedy for instant prayerful experiences, hedonists of the spirit; though I have to add that everyone knows he says that, and often ignores what equally he insists upon, that many are masochists of the spirit who get their kicks out of a sort of spiritual disgruntlement. We want things to go well in prayer, or else we flatter ourselves and self-dramatize that they are going well because it is all so terribly dry and unappetizing a thing; and we are all too ready to be seduced in either case by the same, mistaken notion: that prayer is something which goes on, successfully or otherwise, in our minds, or something we do with them, or some state of mind, whether of feeling, or imagination, or thought. Some of us older ones will even remember being taught to call this prayer in the secrecy of our rooms, 'mental prayer'. And this leads, I think, to false expectations, expectations which live on equally in our delights and in our frustrations with prayer. We are annoyed with ourselves and disillusioned because we cannot get our minds to focus on a single uplifting thought, because our feelings are left high and dry and because our imaginations run picturesque riot. Or else we are pleased with ourselves because we have enjoyed entertaining or encouraging and inspiring thoughts about God. I suppose it is not too dogmatic to say it plainly: thinking about God, feeling good about God, imagining awe-inspiringly divine things have, by themselves, no more power to bring us close to God than has thinking about the shopping, enjoying a Mozart aria or your favourite footballer's latest goal. No more and precisely no less.

But because of the expectation that prayer is, or necessarily involves, having correct thoughts about God or the right feelings, some people – many – find prayer a mental strain. For them – for all of us some of the time – thinking about the shopping is a lot easier, and we cannot often string together two consecutive thoughts about God.

For other people – all of us some of the time – thinking about God on the contrary comes all too easy, it is what they do a lot of the time. Their minds are filled with the eloquent noise of their own thoughts. They are like lecturers declaiming to an audience of one – themselves – as if they were addressing the world. And perhaps they think they are praying – until, that is, they are reminded of the words of the deluded aristocrat who, when asked how he could be so certain that he was Jesus Christ, replied 'But that's easy: it's just that when I pray I find I am talking to myself.'

I wonder if this mistaken notion about prayer is a temptation especially among people of your sort and mine: theologians, preachers, counsellors, pastoral workers and catechists, who professionally, or out of inclination, do a lot of talking about God. Perhaps it is easier for us to be seduced into thinking that making mental speeches about God is a way of speaking to him. It isn't.

But then it is just as hard to be happy with some aspects of the revival of so-called 'contemplative' prayer. It is often given expression, I know, in powerful and richly biblical images of stillness of mind, of inner tranquillity and emotional harmony.

And truly we must obey in some way the command to 'Be still and know that I am God' (Psalm 46.10); true enough, 'My soul is silent towards God alone' (Psalm 62) and we must 'be quiet, wait for God, be patient' (Psalm 37). It is true that we must achieve an interior silence. And I am sure that it is good for us to practise techniques which will help us to be more recollected, more patient mentally, more concentrated in mind and feeling. And for all I know (though I confess that I have not tried), it helps to spend time emptying the mind of its noisiest occupants; for all I know it may help to recite mantras in mentalese and to listen to your own breathing. It is certainly true that John of the Cross held that mentally active prayer is a preliminary stage and that infused, properly contemplative, prayer is a stage beyond it, is wordless prayer, prayer without thought.

All these things I concede as possibly sound applications of those biblical texts, but none of them are what prayer is, nor are they at all necessary means to prayer.

For, just because prayer is not the occurrence of a particular set of thoughts or feelings, not an activity of mind, it does not follow that it is an inactivity of mind, possible only in the absence of thoughts and feelings. Just because prayer is 'passive' it does not follow that you are not praying 'contemplatively' when your mind or feelings are active, indeed when they are hyperactive, in a disorganized, uncontrollable clamour. For the passivity of true prayer has nothing whatever to do with passivity in our mental states: it neither is that condition nor does it require it.

Besides, if there are reasons why it is nonetheless good for us to achieve states of mental and emotional quiet, there are also dangers in it of self-deception and smugness. There are some who are made so anxious by the experience of their own mental chaos that they make a goal for themselves out of mental and emotional 'peace of mind' – a peace which is only a self-creation of the mind and so is a 'peace of this world'. And any peace which the world gives is always a settling for something short of the peace which Jesus gives us. It is the peace of those who have come to terms with themselves and have become reasonably happy with themselves. We must not strive for this peace. The danger is that we will achieve it.

For, just as one mistaken form of prayer consists in straining to think, so another – this pursuit of mental quiet – consists in straining not to think. Personally, I have come to fear the temptation of emotional and mental tidiness and order, sought for as a goal or even as a condition of praying. The man who had a devil cast out of him swept his house clean, tidied and dusted his emotional, mental and moral life and, I suppose, because of that, was satisfied – which is to say that he was occupied by seven devils, 'and the last condition was worse than the first' (Matthew 12.45; Luke 11.26).

Therefore, some rules of thumb:

- You are not praying just because your mind is occupied with thoughts of God, even thoughts addressed to God, or by reflections on the life of Jesus, or by awareness of your dependence on grace, or by feelings of humble self-deprecation.
- But neither are you failing to pray simply because you cannot pull together any such thoughts, when your thoughts drift and scatter like leaves in the wind.
- You are not praying simply because in the presence of such thoughts your feelings are aroused to excitement, or for that matter to a steady, quiet, calm.

- But neither are you failing to pray because, with or without those thoughts, your feelings are stunted and do not flourish.
- You are not praying simply because by nature or by training or technique you have achieved a thoughtless, wordless state of mind, or when you seem, by quiet reflection, to have moved mentally closer to the centre of your soul.

For prayer is not any state of mind at all. That, of course, is why prayer is possible in any state of mind.

Prayer is an act of the will, not of thought or feeling, and we do not understand this because in our modern culture we have intellectually lost touch with any usable meaning of the word; we have come to mean something like a tyrannical force at odds with desire, a force opposed to what we want. It is not surprising therefore that in our personal experience we have lost touch with that power in us which, in older cultures, was called 'will'. For the great spiritual writers of classical and premodern times meant by 'will' some thing more like our deepest desires, or sometimes, our 'hearts': at any rate, the place where our treasure is. And many of those desires lie very deep within us indeed, so that we do not know them, they do not fall within our experience.

Within our experience, what we think, what we feel, and our passions are much closer to the surface than our wills are. We know what we think when we think it, we know what we feel when we feel it, we know those desires which throw themselves at us, we are instantly aware of these things in ourselves. But our wills, our hearts, are a constant mystery to us. Literally, we do not know what we want: we spend much of our lives in ignorance of the deepest movements of desire, unfriendly, unwelcoming to them. Is it any wonder we are so frustrated?

Prayer is the process of discovering in ourselves that with which we can truly love God: that is our will, that is where our hearts are. For 'you have made us for yourself, and our hearts will not rest until they rest in you'. For the same reasons as Augustine, Thomas Aquinas once said of prayer that it is *quodammodo interpretativa voluntatis humanae* – prayer is a kind of revelation to us of what our wills truly are, it is a kind of hermeneutic of the opaque text of desire.

The first step in that process of self-knowledge is also the first step in prayer. It is to learn how to trust absolutely in the love of God for us. And the most immediate effect of that trust is that we will learn how to stop pretending about ourselves, particularly in prayer. This is a quite obvious kind of liberation and has a quite natural kind of attractiveness about it, at least at first, like a sigh of relief at dropping a great weight.

For much of the strain of our earliest efforts to pray derives from our beginning not by praying as we are, but as we think we ought to – under the pressure of models of how we think we should pray.

We mentally adjust our motives to fit the pattern. We begin to see our absurd vanity and, frightened, shrink from it. So we recite the jingles of the humble as if we could smother our vanity with merely pious thoughts. We tell our Father – who in any case sees what we do in secret – that it is not my will that should be done and suppress the sinking feeling that he just might take us at our word. We pretend to be more humble, less bored, less bloody-minded and more in love with God than we really are. We pray not out of ourselves as we really are, but as we think we would pray if we were better than we are, as if the force of mere thought were able to change the reality and truth of ourselves.

Thus do we try to force upon ourselves the aspirations of a 'higher' prayer we are not capable of – not capable of it because it has no reality – and our prayer begins not to strip away, but rather reinforce, our private fantasy-worlds. And do bear this in mind. A prayer which is less than fully honest has a quite alarming capacity to seduce us into a world of its own, to construct and sustain a kind of spiritual unreality and self-obsession. Here, within that self-absorption lie all the possibilities that John of the Cross spoke of, of spiritual self-indulgence on the one hand, on the other, ascetical masochism, plus one other notorious effect appropriate in today's context: that of the unwillingness to drag oneself out of the mere atmospherics, as one might call them, of the prayerful condition, into the real world – as sometimes one can experience at the end of a particularly self-indulgent day of recollection.

All these phenomena are very far from the discovery of our 'wills'; on the contrary, these are the imposition of a false will, one that is not truly our own; and we cannot love God by means of any effort of our own. For if, as Newman tells us, there is a strenuousness of thought which keeps us from our God, nothing does so more insidiously than a corresponding strenuousness of will.

And above all, this effortfulness is a complete failure to trust God. It is the failure to trust him with ourselves as we actually are. It is as if we had to protect God from the truth of ourselves. But in reality it is only we whom we are protecting out of a fear of self-knowledge.

It is the belief that we may only pray if we pray worthily, with the right credentials. So we might as well get it clear from the start: we do not have, we never will have, nor has anyone ever had, the credentials for praying. We do not need them to pray. All we need to know is that our Father in heaven needs us not to have any.

So we might as well pray as we are: as do those who, like the Author of *The Cloud of Unknowing*, pray so much in secrecy that they hide their prayers even from themselves, even from God. They will not even say that they love God very much, because they know that in practice they often love other things more. Nor, always, are you utterly sure that you want to love God more than you do, not, at any rate, at those moments which can sometimes sweep into your life when the terrifying, vertiginous horror of what might be involved hits you. 'There you are, the truth of the matter is that I don't even *want* to love you that much, so it's over to you' is all you can say on such occasions. And you can say it, if you can, because, after all, you do trust in the completely unconditional love which God has for you. That trust is itself prayer, come whatever may into your mind. It is your will's consent, the discovery of where your heart is, the treasure hidden in the field.

En la sua volontade e' nostra pace, say the lowest souls in Dante's *Paradiso*: 'in his will is our peace'. This is the true peace, which if it is to be his peace, and not one of this world, cannot be of our own making. Do not make of your prayer an instrument of your peace, but an opening to his. Which we do if we can make the lesser contribution of that patience which, as Gerard Manley Hopkins says, 'plumes to peace thereafter'.

13

How to be Tempted: A Homily

'Jesus was led up by the Spirit into the wilderness to be tempted by the devil' (Matthew 4.1). But the desert is without form, without feature, arid and barren. Why did Jesus go out to such a place to pray and to be tempted?

Why is it that the Spirit led Jesus there, not for some higher purpose from which he might be tempted, but apparently for no other purpose than to be tempted? Why, from the earliest days of the Church, did our Fathers imitate Jesus and go out into the desert for just the same purpose, to confront the devil in single combat?

Why did the Carthusians and Cistercians in the twelfth century seek out deserts in order to re-establish and renew the *vita apostolica*? Why did John of the Cross describe the 'land of the spirit' as a desert, being, as he put it, 'a land without ways'?

And if all these, and many others among our Christian witnesses, sought deserts to be tempted in, should not we also seek deserts, somehow, in some place? And if so, how and where?

There is a region of ourselves which is a desert, a land of the spirit, unknown to us, because, like a desert it is formless and featureless, and has no obvious characteristics by which we would recognize it. It is a 'land without ways', because there are no obvious routes across it, no signposts, no landmarks. It seems arid and barren, because nothing is born there, nothing grows, everything is burnt up unprotected from the glare of the sun.

Perhaps you will wonder what I am talking about, because I have said both that it is the 'land of the spirit' and that it is the place of temptation, both that it is the place to go to, and that it is dangerous, hostile, unfruitful.

St Teresa of Avila describes the spiritual condition of the smug, those who have arrived in the third mansion of her 'Interior Castle', because they have achieved a measure of self-control, an orderly condition of soul, desire is more or less regulated and will the master. But because they lack humility and self-knowledge, they are self-satisfied prigs. They are relatively temptationless; but have achieved this condition only by confining themselves within carefully defined boundaries of spiritual possibility: their lives, we might add, are sustained in anxiety and threatened by the horizonless dimensions of the desert. Therefore, they know the way all right, for they know how not to get lost in the desert. But as Meister Eckhart warned: 'those who seek God in ways will find ways and lose God'. And because they refuse to follow Jesus into the trackless paths of the desert, there to be tempted, they will never know the land of the Spirit.

Much of what we call 'spirituality' seems to issue from this anxious, threatened, condition of soul. But perhaps such generalization is unfair. Let us at least acknowledge in ourselves the anxiety to become as temptationless as possible, invulnerable to weakness and failure; and let us look, from time to time, at how much work, how much fretting, how much anxiety we invest in the futile pursuit of this invulnerability.

And then let us look at the price we must pay in order to achieve it, a price paid in that contradictory mixture of guilt-ridden self-hatred and vaguely sentimental self-satisfaction, which characterizes so much of our inner life. And then look at the price we make other people pay for such petty victories: our censoriousness, our irritability, our obsessive orderliness, our scrupulosity.

In each of us is this desert; and we devise strategies of avoidance so as to skirt its boundaries: sometimes we use prayer, spiritual exercises, self-denial not, as Jesus did, as what you enter this desert to do, but as ways to avoid entering it, even so as not to notice that it exists.

For there is danger in this desert. The desert is a dangerous place, a threat to us in our desire for mastery, a frustration of our desire to 'be in control', to know the way. And you, are you not training to be priests? Must not you, of all of you, know the way, so as to show others?

Jesus was led by the Spirit into the desert: In telling us this, I suppose Matthew wanted to remind us of Moses, who led the people of Israel for forty years in the desert. Are we told that Moses knew the way? Are we not told that even when he found Mount Sinai, he climbed to the top to see God and there saw only a cloud of unknowing, the darkness of God? Did Jesus himself go in the desert to be given privileged illumination? Jesus was led by the Spirit into the wilderness in order to be tempted by the devil.

If you, who will be priests, wish to show your people the way, first find the way to your own desert, there to be tempted. And if you go there to be tempted, undoubtedly you will often fail. Then 'rejoice', says de Caussade, 'everytime you discover a new defect'.

And if you go there as priests, you will go like Moses, bringing your people with you. This, I suppose, is one of the personal meanings of your priesthood, deeply bound up with its sacramental meaning: that wherever you go, you carry your people with you. And there, in the vulnerability, weakness and failure of your desert, you cannot fail to find Jesus, for there you will find that priest who, although he did not sin, is able 'to sympathize with our weaknesses' and who 'in every respect has been tempted as we are' (Hebrews 4.15). And by the way, have you ever meditated on that phrase: 'in *every* respect tempted as we are', or are you too practically docetistic to contemplate it? Or is it just a personal fear that there are some parts of this desert which, just because you are a priest, you could not dare to admit having visited?

I suppose that this desert is really just the region of self-knowledge and humility. Nor actually is it as grim as all that. In fact, the chief evidence of humility is a sense of humour, particularly about yourself, which I think is the eighth gift of the Holy Spirit. May that same Holy Spirit lead you into the desert, there to laugh at the tempting devil.

14

How to be Distracted

This morning I said that prayer is a matter of the will. Perhaps you would have been happier if I had said that it is a matter of the 'heart', but I do not mind which you say so long as either way what we mean is that prayer touches upon, indeed deeply burrows into, the depths of human desire, there to meet with that with which, truly, we can and do love God. I say 'can and do'. For over and over again we are paralysed by our own effortfulness: we think of loving God as something we have to get ourselves to do, because if we do not get ourselves to do it, we will not love him.

I say, and merely follow Augustine, Meister Eckhart, Julian of Norwich and John of the Cross and so many others who say it, that we are made for God; our whole being loves God, our deepest soul loves God. The trouble is that in our everyday experiencing selves we think we do not love God as much as we should; which is exactly why it does not matter what our minds are saying to us. For our problem is that we live out of touch with that in us which loves God, there is a barrier between us and that intimacy of ourselves where the love of God 'stirs and boils and seethes', as Meister Eckhart put it; for 'you, o God, are more intimate to me than I am to myself', as Augustine says, adding: 'You were within me, but I was outside myself.' For, 'in every soul that is to be saved', says Julian, 'there is a Godly will, that never consents to sin, and never shall'. And when we are out of touch with that depth in us, that 'will', the barrier between that depth in which we do love God and our doubting selves is little other than our own effort, born of the desire to be the ones who pull it off. By contrast with that love of God which God himself has placed in us, the love of God which is our own achievement is, simply, a fake.

So if prayer is a matter of the will, the last thing it is is a matter of self-will. 'When we cry, "Abba! Father!", it is the Spirit himself bearing witness with our spirit that we are children of God' (Romans 8.15–16). Perhaps it is not too extreme to say: We can never say 'I prayed to God', for if I did it, it was not prayer and if it was prayer, then the Spirit did it.

Of course the Spirit bears witness, as Paul says, with our spirit, it is in and through us that the Spirit prays and this is the paradox: since it is in and through our freedom that the Spirit prays, the prayer of the Spirit within us is more our own act than any other act could possibly be. For that is most ours which is most free.

But prayer is never our act as distinct from the work of the Spirit within us, it is our act only as one with the work of the Spirit within us, when our spirit and the Holy Spirit are, as Bernard of Clairvaux used to say, *unus spiritus*. For there is only one prayer, and that is the prayer of the Father to the Son and of the Son to the Father, and that prayer is called by the name of the Spirit. That is why, incidentally, the first and principal prayer of Christians is the prayer of the Church: for the Church is the Spirit in our history and time and experience. For our part, we pray only in so far as the Spirit prays in us. We cannot add to that prayer by any prayer of our own. We can only consent to the work of prayer within us. For the prayer that is within us is the Trinity itself, dwelling within us.

What is more, even that free consent is the work of the Spirit. For the very freedom by which we consent to grace is itself the work of grace. As Thomas Aquinas says: 'God does not justify us without our involvement, for it is by an act of free will that we consent to the justice with which he justifies us. But that act of free will is the effect of grace, not its cause: for which reason, the whole action [of our justification] is the work of grace.'

That is why Jan van Ruusbroec can say, echoing those famous words of Augustine: 'God is truly more within us than we are ourselves, and his inward driving or working in us, natural or supernatural, is more within us and closer to us than are our own works; and therefore God works in us from within outwards, and all creatures work from without inwards.'

'God works from within outwards' – that is to say, that in which the Spirit prays is our freedom, for our freedom is what is most within us, it is what we mean by our 'wills' or our 'hearts', for that it is with which we can love God. But the freedom with which we love God is itself the work of God's love. And that work is already done: it was work done from all eternity, in the eternal birth of our selves in God. We, for our part, have lost touch with that selfhood, that freedom, that 'heart', where God loves God by means of our love.

But is not all this a form of 'quietism', even of fatalism? It is true that prayer is always the work of God. It is true that many do not pray at all, and many of us do but unwillingly and few pray 'constantly', as Paul asks us to. But if prayer is simply gift, already given, never won, either we have it or we don't, so either way there is nothing to be done.

The conclusion does not follow and is false. To be a Christian at all is to be called to live by the life of God itself. How do we know that God wants us to reach so high? We know this because God cannot possibly want anything else. God is all love. Love is an absolute necessity to God. He can do nothing to any other end or by any other means. So I repeat: prayer is always given us, at every time and in every place. It is simply we who have lost touch with it.

Being incapable of anything but love he cannot do anything but pour himself out over his creatures in sheer love of them, and he cannot have any difficulty in loving us, because there is nothing in God to cause a difficulty.

This truth is utterly incomprehensible to us. However important we may think we think love to be, we cannot in fact comprehend the idea of a person living by no other means at all; for we will trust to love up to a point, but will take out an insurance policy of utility, good planning, a modicum of self-interest, or whatever, just in case. And besides its being incomprehensible, frankly we do not in any case believe it, which is why we try to make out to God that we are not quite as unlovable as we think, very deep down, we are. That need arises only out of a deeply rooted hatred and rage with ourselves, a feeling God cannot possibly share. For 'it is his delight to play with the children of men'. As Thomas says again: 'God does us good without any restraint and out of sheer delight, not because there could possibly be anything in it for him.'

It is in our will and hearts, therefore, that is to say, within our freedom, that this prayer, this exchange of love, does its work. That is why that silence which is, as it were, the method by which the work of prayer is done, is not some psychological state of calm or quiet in our thoughts and feelings; nor does it consist in some special experience of God. As I said to you this morning, there is nothing which we have to be feeling or thinking in order to be praying, nor is there anything which we have not to be thinking or feeling in order to be praying; prayer is simply a matter of what we are seeking and consenting to.

And it is the undividedness, the singleness, of that seeking and consenting which is the silence, or desert, in which alone prayer can take place. It is in our heart's not being distracted from the search for God alone, as the Author of *The Cloud of Unknowing* puts it, for God as he is in himself and not for anything we can get out of him; it is the life of 'yearning for God' of Ruusbroec, it is 'my spirit seeking you, my flesh fainting for you' of the Psalmist, it is 'the deer which pants for the rivers' – it is the unbounded unconditional desire for God, it is the refusal to live by any other means than love itself. It is a 'silence' because it is an utter steadfastness in love. And because of this, it is a dissatisfaction with anything we can rely on short of love: and this dissatisfaction is not something we have to learn. I am not offering you a prescription for action. I am not saying, 'Learn how to hate the world or yourselves.' On the contrary, I am offering you a diagnosis. For we are already dissatisfied: that, for sure, we know; we already hate the world and ourselves quite enough as it is.

For our hearts are divided. This heart of ours has layer upon layer of desire, some light, some dark, some translucent with honesty and integrity, others opaque with self-love, resentment and despair. Desire is entangled in a forest of ambiguity, of 'willing and partly willing', of mixed motive and feeling – this is the true *regio dissimilitudinis*, the 'land of unlikeness' of which the ancient monastic tradition used to speak. Here, in this land, we cannot be fully happy: all the complaint of our unhappiness lies in this dividedness and in our attachment to it, in our unwillingness to live in that land of the self where the love of God already dwells within us, unrecognized and unbefriended. We actually prefer the half-light of ambiguous desire, frightened by too much love.

Hence it is, that when in prayer we begin to approach more nearly to this source of our being there is provoked in us a riot and a rebellion and an outcry in our feelings and thought and hopes, for we are unsettled in those comforting complicities with our half-world of partial happiness. Our ambiguities of desire are, as it were, 'outed', and the look of them seems ugly. Prayer, for most of the time, can consist in little else than a trusting acceptance of that chaos, for that is the stability of our being in God, a stability which can never be captured in thought, is never felt and never needs to be. Learning how to pray without the reassurance of appropriate thoughts and feelings, this is otherwise called 'faith' – or if you like, it is a 'dark night' or a 'cloud of unknowing' or the 'desert' in which Jesus went out to pray in order to be tempted, as the Gospel says. For don't forget, that desert, that land of the spirit, is, as John of the Cross put it, 'a land without ways'.

A word, therefore, about distractions in prayer. I think we are wrong to slap them down, for they are a rare opportunity for our getting to know ourselves, getting to know where our hearts are. As Herbert McCabe once said, no one is distracted from what they really want: the drowning man's prayer for rescue is rarely visited by distractions. But our prayer is often distracted *by* what we really want: which might suggest that our prayer lacks the urgency of the drowning man because it lacks reality, it doesn't connect with our actual desires.

So it seems a pity if we find ourselves fighting distractions as if they were the enemy of prayer. We dislike them, because we like to feel in control, and distractions make us feel wretchedly at their mercy. We do so want to feel that we are praying and distractions spoil the feel. Which, of course, is why, on the contrary, we ought to listen to them and pray with them, not against them. For distractions are the effects of prayer, they are how prayer reveals to us where lies the land of the heart, they are the material of what Thomas called the 'hermeneutic of desire'. They tell us about what we really want.

And could I make here a comment on a particularly contemporary form of high-mindedness about petitionary prayer. Simon Tugwell has pointed out that until about the thirteenth century it was taken for granted that the Latin *oratio* meant asking God for things. From the thirteenth century on, however, this notion of prayer as petition was superseded by something thought to be higher than it, 'contemplative' prayer, or some such. Moreover, the feeling grows, and in some circles today dominates, that you ought only to pray for worthy things, and Herbert McCabe, again, reports on the theological liberal who, on hearing that the plane is about to crash, thinks it unworthy to pray that it won't and grimly prays only to accept the will of God. That, I think, is a classic case of decent prayer being distracted by bad theology, indeed by a kind of spiritual snobbery.

For my part, I prefer to go along with Augustine and Thomas, who, commenting on Jesus' prayer in the garden of Gethsemane, declare it to show that it is perfectly legitimate to pray for whatever one wants, even if one knows it to be contrary to the will of God. Nor only legitimate. I repeat. Unless you pray for what you actually want, you will never learn what you really want, you will never learn that truth of yourself out of which alone prayer is efficacious. Therefore, do not adjust your wants – however small-minded and mean you think they are – to your preconceived model of worthy prayer. It is what God gives you in response to your most miserably petty desires, if only they are admitted, which will transform your desires into something more worthy. All the rest is your pretence, born of an unhappiness with what you are and what you dislike yourself for desiring. No wonder such prayer is distracted.

So be happy with distractions. Or at the very least have a sense of humour about them. If, after a period of really useless prayer you can laugh with God at the frustrated ego and its disappointments, you will not have wasted your time.

For all I have said to you amounts to this: if we can manage nothing else in prayer we can manage patience, perseverance and trust. In the lovely phrase of Simone Weil, prayer is a 'waiting for God'. It is a waiting with our wants placed in the presence of his wants: and from that waiting emerges, ever so slowly, a wanting that he should do it, whatever 'it' is.

That complete and total trust in nothing but God is a silence in our wills, the desert into which we follow Jesus so as to pray. It is a silence which the Spirit ever deepens in us, expands, and makes continuous with our lives – continuous and quite compatible with our frenzied and hyperactive business, with our neurotically anxious minds, with our tempted, fraught hearts, with the chaotic riot of imagination, with our aimless and misdirected feelings. And so it will not matter what psychological noise is the necessary accompaniment of our lives, for that silence is always an unapproachable, unfelt depth within the noise. As it was put once by one who knows best about silence, an anonymous Carthusian monk, the Word to whom we listen in prayer was generated in the depths of the Father's silence. And it is in that same Father's silence that we listen for the Word. The silence in our hearts is our sharing in the life of the Father, so that in that silence – his and ours – that same Word is generated in us too; thus may we live by the Spirit.

When I got to this point in preparing this talk it occurred to me that you might think of it as being hopelessly spiritual. That would be altogether to miss the point. This is no higher, mystical doctrine.

I am a layman, and life is so frenetically busy that I am in sympathy mainly with Teresa of Avila who complained to God about the mystical happenings he visited upon her when she had urgent letters to write. I have only wanted to say one thing negatively and one thing positively. The negative thing concerns what prayer is not, the models of praying which prevent its sincerity: it is not something you do, a practice you can master or a describable experience you can learn the techniques for generating; but then, neither is it an indescribable experience, a higher, mystical state, a higher inwardness, a rapture, a sense of union with the beyond-experience, or any such. Prayer is neither a describable experience nor an indescribable experience, and this is because it is not any sort of 'experience' at all. If it were any sort of experience it would be exclusive of other sorts of experience and excluded by them, and it is for thinking that that many cannot understand or practise Paul's simple instruction to 'pray always' (Ephesians 6.18). Well, I wanted to set before you an account of our prayer with Jesus 'in the desert' which would be compatible and continuous with the mind's being turned towards the immediate and pressing need of another, or of work, or one's sexual activity, or of politics: for the desert in which we can pray is present in all these things, as a depth of silence in which the Word is generated: if only we can find access to that desert in ourselves.

And the positive thing I wanted to say was that prayer is our consent to the love of God, a consent which we give regardless of what we experience in giving it. That consent is the gift of grace. We cannot experience that grace itself; but what the Spirit gives us as grace we can experience as freedom. It is, after all, in that freedom that the children of God can cry 'Abba! Father!'

15

Waiting for the Spirit

Today, of course, is the Sunday before the Feast of the Ascension. It is 'before' not just in terms of secular time, but also liturgically. For the tenor of the readings is distinctly that of waiting, of anticipation, for the Spirit. And that is the meaning of the ascension. We are waiting for the Spirit, who will come only when Jesus goes.

Which means that he goes, but also that he does not go. For the Holy Spirit is the spirit of Jesus; he goes in his limited, physical, historical and so distant way, so as to be able to stay in an unlimited, immediate and intimate way; therefore, he is, when he comes in the Holy Spirit, not less but more present than if he had not ascended.

And when, in two weeks' time we celebrate Pentecost, we will have completed the whole meaning of the resurrection. By then it will have been forty days since Easter, forty days in which we celebrate the whole, complex meaning of the resurrection as it were in liturgically separate bits: the shock of the empty tomb, the surprise of the appearances to the women, to the disciples at Emmaus, to the apostles; his departure and the waiting for the coming of the Holy Spirit, the coming of the Holy Spirit and the preaching of the gospel in many tongues. All these, set out serially, form the liturgical pattern; and I suppose there is a sort of pedagogy in this narrative which separates out the different meanings of Easter; but there is learning only in our putting them all together again, in our seeing each element as getting its meaning from all the others and as adding up to just one thing: the meaning of the resurrection of Jesus.

Thus we wait for the Holy Spirit. And the Holy Spirit comes. But when the Holy Spirit comes, still we are waiting. And just as each moment in the forty-day celebration of Easter is simultaneous with the other, so are the waiting for the Spirit and the coming of the Spirit all the same one thing, though we experience them differently.

Which is why, if you are at all like me the waiting seems much more real than the coming. I think we know all about the waiting. But when did he come to us? How are we supposed to know?

Jesus says: 'the world cannot receive' this Spirit, 'since it neither sees nor knows him' (John 14.17). And then he says 'but you know him'. Do I? I don't think so. Is this just 'worldliness' on my part? You, on the other hand, must speak for yourselves.

Well, there are those who say that they know the Spirit. They will tell you that they are filled with him, that they receive him, together with their fellow Christians, in inspirational moments of worship, or prayer, or whatever. And maybe they do. Or rather, for sure they do, but maybe not in that form and mode in which they believe they do.

For the Spirit is our friend, but he – or she, if you prefer – is also a Stranger. He moves where he wills. Where he wills. Not when or where we will. He is hidden. He is 'mystical', for that is the root meaning of the word 'mystical' – 'hidden'.

So it is not surprising, really, that so much of our Christian lives seem filled with absence, non-experience, non-knowing and, relative to some of our expectations, disappointment. So, where is this 'Consoler'? The Author of *The Cloud of Unknowing* tells us that it is those who want the experience of God, of the Spirit, who are living 'outside' themselves, in the world, who will translate the coming of the Spirit into the terms of their own experience. They will get the Spirit they deserve, the spirit limited by the limitations of their own experience.

So, among those who belong to 'the world' and 'do not know' the Spirit, are perhaps those of us who are despondent that we never experience him; but also those who are excessively cheerful because they are certain that they do; for neither recognize the Spirit who 'is with you, [who] is in you' (John 14.17). Both, we could say, fear the risk of faith and would rather have the reassurance of their own experience.

We are not 'worldly' because we do not have sensations of the Spirit within us. We are worldly because we are disappointed and discouraged that we don't.

In his *Confessions*, St Augustine describes in vivid detail how he searched for God in his youth and into his early maturity, and altogether, as he thought, without success. His story, until his conversion, is that of a deeply unhappy man, a man of profound desire profoundly unsatisfied. A man who became more unsettled, more erratic and vulnerable emotionally, the nearer his desire came to God.

He asks himself: How could I have been seeking God, if, in my ignorance, I did not know what God was? When I search for a friend in a crowd I know whom I am looking for, I do not know where he is, but I know who he is, I can describe him.

When I search for God, it is not the same: It is not, as we might think, that I know how to recognize God, but do not know where he is, that we have temporarily lost sight of him, though we think we know enough about God to be sure that we will recognize him when he is around.

But we don't know how to recognize God, not *that* way. So often we miss him because we do not know how to wait. When he was 'converted', what Augustine discovered was not that he had finally learned what God was like, so he could spot him now at a glance. It was not as if he had been looking for someone unknown to him in a crowd but under the wrong description and so could not find him; and then, given the right description, could pick him out.

It was more like a person who has been starved of love, who has never experienced love in his life, who can be said to be 'looking for love'. He doesn't know what love is like, not so as to have experienced it much. But all the same, he will know it when he finds it; when he finds it he will be able to say, 'all the time that is what I was looking for'. But he did not know it in the seeking.

But then, Augustine says: 'You were within me, but I was outside myself.' When the children playing in the garden in Milan sing *Tolle lege, tolle lege*, 'take it and read, take it and read', Augustine breaks down in tears, because now he knows what he could always have known: that God, the Spirit, was not there 'all the time' distantly in some far off object which he could not reach. The Spirit was there all the time in the seeking itself, in the desire for God, in the disappointment at not finding him, in the unhappiness of unsatisfied desire, in the very intensity of the desire for God.

And this is the nature of the Spirit: to be a Stranger, always one step away from us. Always one step behind us. Always one step in front of us. Always eluding us, but always within us, 'more within us than we are ourselves', as Augustine puts it. Never absent, in spite of the absence of our experience of him, present, perhaps, in the very experience of absence.

This, I think, sounds all very mystical, perhaps all too mystical. How I hate preaching, for I have some wrong-headed notion, hard to eradicate, that preachers are supposed to tell people what to do, and I prefer the teacher's business of helping people to understand.

So, just to ensure that I have fulfilled my bargain with our chaplain, Fr Michael, let me tell you something, something that you ought not to do. Do not ever look for the Spirit within yourself otherwise than you look for him in other people. For the Spirit is love. God is all love. God cannot do anything, Thomas Aquinas says, in a spirit of mean self-advancement, cannot do anything for any other purpose, or by any other means, than love.

That is the divine omnipotence: because God can only love he can do all things. That too is the divine unknowability, what I like to call 'the darkness of God': the darkness of God, the 'cloud of unknowing' in which God is wrapped, is an inaccessible light, pure transparent love. If there were anything else in God but love, some power which derived from something other than love, we would be able to see it, comprehend it, grasp it, like a shadow in the light, opaque enough to be seen.

But, because of sin, we are unable to rely on nothing else but love. For sure, we think that love is an important thing, in fact we may think we think that love is the most important thing. But we will not permit ourselves the risk of relying on nothing else at all. We take out insurance policies just in case love lets us down, we pay our premiums to power, or intelligence, or cunning, or money, or friends, or influence or whatever. So, for us, we will love up to a point, beyond which we think it necessary to be realistic.

But Jesus did not. He was the perfect image of the Father and he came to dwell with us. The world – us, because we are sinful – cannot bear this image of pure love, and hates it. It had to kill Jesus, for he was in the end unbearable – as is any revelation which exposes us so completely to our need to compromise love. That is the message of Jesus' life among us, and of our lives among one another, that the price of too much love is death.

That love for one another is demanded of us in unexpected places, at surprising times, coming like a thief in the night, it steals up on us just when we think that we have everything in ourselves in place, organized, secure, the entirely regrettable condition of moral rectitude.

Jesus told the parable of a man who had a devil cast out of his soul. No doubt delighted and relieved, the man tidied up his soul, swept it out quite clean, put everything back in order, whereupon the devil cast out returned with seven devils to occupy him, and the last condition of the man 'was worse than the first' (Matthew 12.45;

Luke 11.26). So much for the vanity of human hopes and plans. I think that story could be thought of as a story of the person who looks for the Spirit in himself, as the place of privileged access. So I say again: the Spirit is the love which binds us together in bonds of charity; that is why if you cannot find the Spirit in every other person, whatever you do find within yourself, it will not be the Spirit of Jesus.

So in waiting for the Spirit, the position is exactly the opposite of the person who knows whom he is looking for but does not know where he is; we know where the Spirit is to be found, but my goodness does he sometimes take unrecognizable forms!

And Augustine was right that the place of the Spirit is 'within'; but you will recognize him within yourself only in the same way and to the same extent that you recognize him within the needs of others: in their poverty, and weakness, and inadequacy, and fears – in short, in their unexpected, or tiresome or excessively demanding need for you.

Our whole lives are therefore lives lived in the expectation of the unexpected, we live, as Christians, in this condition of waiting, open to every possibility of demand; but we will as often as not be unprepared when it comes, for we never know when that Spirit will surprise us. We wait for the Spirit, therefore, but he always comes, for the Spirit is already in our waiting. Which is why the whole reality of the resurrection is found in both at once: in the waiting and in the coming, for the waiting is in the coming and the coming is in the waiting.

So, today, we celebrate the whole reality of Easter, as we do every Sunday; but today, as it were, we celebrate Easter from the standpoint of the waiting which it creates in us, that lovely waiting which is fulfilled in the surprise of meeting the Spirit, when we least expect it, in one another.

Must we not thus ever wait. For the Son of man will come when we least expect. And 'when he comes will he find [us] ready?' (see Matthew 24.44; Luke 12.40).

16

Praying and Eating

When, after his resurrection, Jesus appears to his disciples and wishes to prove that he is alive, he eats a fish. So Luke tells us. No doubt a Patristic or a medieval commentator would have offered much ingenuity, if not what we might think of as wisdom, on the significance of its being a fish that Jesus ate. But perhaps we should be less exercised by the particular dietary significance, and more by the connection made between being alive and eating. Whatever else the resurrection of Jesus means, it means being alive. And for Jesus to be alive is for Jesus to be a human being. And for Jesus to be a living human is for Jesus to be alive in his body. That, and that alone is how Jesus could be alive, doing things like eating a fish. So I should say, at any rate, though I do know of Christians who want to avoid the difficulties which arise from saying that.

For there are those who prefer to say that after the resurrection Jesus is alive in the Spirit, and so not in his body; perhaps in the faith of Christians, which is how the Spirit is present among us; perhaps in the analogical, the spiritual body, which is the Church and in its faith, and perhaps in its preaching and witness. Which is, of course, all true, except for the '. . . and so not . . .': in the Spirit and so not in the body. If we really mean that it is Jesus who is raised, then a human being is now alive: and a human being cannot be alive in the Spirit if he is not alive in his body. It cannot be a question of one claim being set against the other, alive in faith, or alive in his body. But it is a question of one claim being dependent on the other: if not alive in his body then not alive in faith, or in the Spirit, or in the Church. Therefore, Jesus eats a fish, in order that we may know what to believe about the resurrection: it has something to do with our being bodies.

There is some significance also in its being eating whereby Jesus shows us he is a living human person. Jesus, or at least the Jesus we know of from the evangelists, evidently gave a lot of thought to eating, and attached great significance to it, especially to parties. How a person thinks about parties, he appears to say, tells you a great deal about how that person thinks about the kingdom – which is one word for it; another word for it is the resurrection. There are people who have better things to do with their time than to go to parties – their interests are too narrowly and selfishly confined, they always have businesses to run, or family obligations to see to first. They are always preoccupied: that is to say, other things than such time-wasting celebrations as our evensong here, for example, always take priority. So, Jesus says, they'll not be invited next time. Others will go to parties, but cannot be bothered to dress appropriately: throw them out, he says. Others are ill-mannered and offer grudging and mean hospitality: *utquid perditio haec*, they say, like Judas: 'Why this waste?' – but Jesus praises the nameless woman, who spends without conscience. Others only go to parties they will be important at: publicly humiliate them, Jesus says.

Parties, Jesus implies, are not transactions: they are gifts. You don't qualify to be invited. You can't be too busy to receive a gift. You don't look a gift horse in the mouth; but neither do you resent its expense. Gratitude for a gift consists first in receiving it well, not first in thoughts of returning the gift. But parties are gifts of food and drink; and when we humans offer one another food and drink we offer one another the gift of life.

Because human life is bodily, and bodily life depends on food and drink, the gift of food and drink is the root symbol of the gift of life. So Jesus' eating a fish is not just a sort of proof of his bodily resurrection, it declares its meaning. Perhaps one part of that meaning does, after all, have to do specifically with fish. Of course it is hard to know what to say about Jesus' bodily presence after his resurrection. But whatever we are to say about Jesus' body, he returns to his disciples in *their* material bodily particularity, in their mortal condition as fishermen. Jesus' joining them in eating a fish, therefore, is an acknowledgement and an affirmation of their carnality, their temporality, their material particularity. But if that significance can be derived concerning the disciples' bodiliness – that it is not yet raised, that it remains a body mortal – what are we to say of Jesus' bodiliness, how are we to conceive of that?

Are we to say that Jesus' body, after the resurrection, is not really a body, it is a sort of hybrid, a weightless, thinned-out, not very material thing, rather like a ghost (as we might suppose Paul to have meant when he spoke of the resurrection body as a spiritual body in his first letter to the Corinthians)? Well, hardly. I do not know of any theological account of the resurrection of the body in such terms as doubt its true nature as a body, which does not involve gross conceptual muddles. Rather than confusing us about the nature of the human body by the introduction of a very odd, conceptually indefensible, special case of it, the resurrection ought, on the contrary, to clarify what we mean by the human body by revealing to us something deeper, something we might otherwise not have understood, about the body's true nature, about its reality.

For our bodies are how we are present to one another. Our bodies are how we speak to one another. We might say, the human body is human language. If you find this a difficult idea, or just a bit too materialistic a thing to say about language, then ask yourself: what else but matter is capable of bearing, or conveying, meaning? What are words spoken but sounds, noises which have meaning? What are words written, but marks on a surface which can be read? What else are gestures, but bodily movements which say something? I know we are apt to think of bodies as bits of matter, and of meanings as bits of mind. And that is all right so long as we don't find ourselves denying that how we human beings are meaningfully present to one another is through our material bodies: we know one another's minds through bodily meanings, as Jesus revealed himself to his disciples: by eating fish with them.

Now if we ask, how did Jesus communicate with his disciples, when after the resurrection he appeared to them in the room, we are asking how does the resurrection itself – 'the kingdom' as we otherwise call it – speak to us. That is to say, we are asking how is that kingdom present to us, here, now, in our temporality, in our carnality and mortality, in our equivalently mortal condition, as it were, of being fishermen? And the answer has to be the same as before: the kingdom is present to us as bodies speak to bodies, as eating fish together communicates something. And if you will go that far with me, then you will not find it hard to conclude that that answer points us towards the Eucharist: it is in eating and drinking together, in that sharing with one another the gift of life, that there is present among us the gift of new life, our mortal bodies sharing in, or as we say, communicating in, the immortal body, the eternal Word, the resurrection, spoken to us in the form of food.

For the resurrection of Jesus does not diminish his bodiliness. It fulfils it: we might say that it radicalizes it. In his natural life, Jesus' presence was limited by time and space and contingency, for his

body was thus limited. We should not say: Jesus' presence, his avail-
ability, his power to communicate, was limited by his body. We
should say rather: his power to communicate was limited by his
body's mortality, by its being a 'body of death'. Therefore, by over-
coming death, Jesus' body was released from its limitations; and so,
raised by his Father to immortality, he was more present to his
disciples in the room when he ate a fish, than he had been when, on
the hillside, he multiplied loaves and fishes – not less. He is more
present to us now than he could have been to us had we walked with
him on the shores of Lake Galilee – not less. And so he is more
bodily now, as raised, not less, than before his death: this presence
of mine, he said to his disciples, is not that of a ghost.

Now to say all this is to cast some doubt on a contemporary
assumption – one which, I should say, can look more like a prejudice
– concerning the authority of immediate personal experience. We
think of personal experience as unmediated by anything so impersonal and distanced as doctrine. It is the assumption which is
contained in that lingering moment of wishful-thinking which lurks
in the thought of how decisive it would have been to meet the person
of the historical Jesus, of how immediately convincing that would
have been, by comparison with the historically distanced figure we
find in the Scriptures, or in the doctrinally and theologically mediated
reality of the Eucharist or service of prayer. It is that same wishful-
thinking which leads some to be more excited by the witness of the
Shroud of Turin, or the experience of the Holy Places, than by their
own, often uninspiring, experience of Christian worship. It is there,
in more theological form, in the thought that such is the priority of
the personal and immediate experience, that faith itself has to be
reconfigured as being a kind of immediate and personal experience.
In which case we should remind ourselves that in his natural life
Jesus was not all that convincing. More perceptive people than you
and I had serious doubts about his credentials, thought some of his
claims for himself pretty outrageous, and most honest people could
not see in him that revelation of his Father's will that he declared
himself to be fulfilling. In fact, in the end, hardly anyone could see
anything but a disappointment. So we should not count on our
having been any better impressed by Jesus, had we been there to
meet him in person before his death, than we are by meeting him in
person in the Eucharist after his resurrection.

Which, after all, we do in faith and as it were in eating fish, in our bodies; what we eat becomes word, no longer just our word, spoken among ourselves, but the Word, spoken to us by the Father in the Son, the word which promises our resurrection. For the Word made flesh in Jesus becomes the flesh made Word in us. That is our resurrection, a mystery of faith, beyond all experience. 'Thomas', Jesus said, 'you believe because you have seen. Blessed are those who have not seen, and yet believe' (see John 20.29).

The Intellectual Love of God

The first of the sermons which follow was preached in October 2001 at Evensong in Jesus College Chapel, Cambridge. I knew that three of the best doctoral students I have ever supervised would be there, and I preached as if to them, though they did not know it then. The second sermon is a University Sermon preached in the University Church of Our Lady the Virgin, Oxford, in May 2002, and I wrote it and then rewrote it afterwards with the assistance of several of my PhD students, two of whom had been at the sermon in Jesus College. What, very inadequately, I try to explain in these sermons is something about the relationship of teaching and learning which I share with those and many other students, a mutual, reciprocal relationship; at any rate, the sermons arise out of that relationship and are wholly indebted to the significance it has for me. That relationship is the thing I am most grateful for in all my career as an academic theologian, and especially to them, who truly know what it is to learn.

17

Loving God with your Mind

It occurred to me to say a few words this evening about the spiritual possibilities of intellect. Not, to be sure, about the spiritual possibilities available to intellectuals, possibilities which they might exploit alongside their intellectual lives, but by other means than intellect; even less about the spiritual possibilities one might seek in spite of intellect, as some do, finding the demands of intellect to be a spiritual embarrassment. I wondered if one might speak of the spiritual possibilities of intellect itself. The other sermons seemed not too difficult to write, but as to a spirituality which lies within what you and I do with so much preoccupation day in and day out, one is forced to wonder whether we possess any longer, as once we did, a sense of 'intellect' which bears within it a spirituality of its own. So I wrote this sermon as a start. But I am afraid it is one you will have to finish for yourselves. For it ends, you might say, on a false note.

One bit, at least, is easy. We all know of ways in which intellect can be a despiriting force, of intellect's capacity to betray the gifts of grace and of love which have been given to us; we all know how intellect can, to use Jeremiah's image, play the harlot, unloosen bonds of loyalty, how it can cynically destabilize mind and heart through a sort of promiscuity of thought. We know of the spiritually destructive power of intellect, because we know how it can, through an excess of self-consciousness, evacuate selfhood, paralyse emotion, and feed a debilitating self-obsession. We know of these things if only theoretically from Hegel's pathology of what he called 'the unhappy consciousness', that hyperactivity of thought and its consequent condition of emotional deracination and objectlessness. In any case, perhaps we know what Hegel means because we have experienced it, if not in others, then at least in ourselves, as that common condition of intellectuals – their proneness to depression, their chronic sadness.

For this 'unhappy consciousness' is a paralysis of self-reflection, like the predicament of the centipede, which has no difficulty co-ordinating one hundred legs at a time on condition that it does not think *how* it can be done. An excess of reflection is an excess of seeing, and an excess of seeing is an excess of light, it is the condition of too much transparency. It is the mentality of the cynic, for whom nothing is seen because everything is seen through, depriving the world of density; it is like a flash of lightning which first oversaturates the world with light, draining it of colour, only to leave behind it a darkness deeper than before. Who, writing a doctoral thesis, or otherwise being engaged in long-term intellectual endeavours, has not been afflicted by episodes of such feeling, and does not understand all too well the warning of the Angel to Gerontius in Newman's poem: 'It is thy very strenuousness of thought which keeps thee from thy God'?

Nor is this pathology only the alienated personal condition of intellectuals, for it as much characterizes cultures as persons – our culture, at any rate, which some declare to be 'postmodern'. And I suppose it is not surprising, after all, that among some academics there should prevail a mentality for which nothing simply 'presents' itself as given, for which 'presence', as they call it, is endlessly postponed, set in retreat down an endless chain of 'othernesses' without destination or goal; at least I suppose it is not so surprising if there are some who propose these things, given a culture which has pushed out the boundaries of the market so as to enclose all cultural and moral – even spiritual – values, and converts them as values into what they will exchange with. Postmodernism is but the market reconceived as intellect: though one does wonder, sometimes, whether what its advocates describe is truly our cultural condition and is not rather their own condition of alienation from it.

Either way, this is intellect playing the harlot, it is intellect without loyalties; and for the theologian it is the harlotry of Judah, not of Israel, the harlotry not of those who are faithless and turn away from God to their carnal pleasures, but the harlotry of those who are false, who return to God 'but in pretence', for they play at fidelity with words, and have nothing in their hearts (Jeremiah 3.10). Perhaps it is those of us who are theologians who know this best, because it is intellect's proximity to spirit, the very closeness in which much thinking about God may seem to stand to a true sharing of mind in the divine life itself, which gives theology its special power to corrupt and betray – displacing spirit, through caricature, with the mimicry of thought. Thus is this harlotry, this betrayal, as Jeremiah tells us, an idolatry.

Well, as the spiritual possibilities of intellect go, I suppose that is the easy, because negative, bit. But the negativity is too facile as it stands, for such an attitude but serves to feed an easy-going spiritual philistinism, an anti-intellectualism, the brainless spirituality of those who hope for the salvation of their souls on condition of unsaved minds, the love of God on condition of an impoverished vision. Of course intellect is dangerous, as sex is dangerous, so the fear of both is understandable. But fear of intellect is vastly more dangerous spiritually than intellect, just as, more famously, the fear of sex is more spiritually dangerous than sex. We say, conventionally, that, out of fear of sex, Christians often do not know how to love God with their bodies; we say less often than we should, that, out of fear of intellect, Christians do not know how to love God with their minds: they seem merely puzzled at the thought of what Spinoza called 'the intellectual love of God'.

So, if we want to find a meaning for the word 'spirit' – and I do not think we have to hand a serviceable meaning for it – we must find it where the ancients found it, in some meaning, bearing on what we academics do and live by, for Spinoza's phrase: 'the intellectual love of God'. And that means we need to recover something of that ancient meaning of 'intellect' which will allow for a sense of an intellectual love, or, to use a phrase modish in some Cambridge theological circles, an *eros* of intellect. For it was on account of his thinking of intellect's endless searchings as being driven by desire for its source in God that Augustine was able to think of 'mind' and 'spirit' as virtual synonyms; just as, on account of our inability to conceive of the mind's being a form of love, we are constrained to think of 'intellectual love' as virtually an oxymoron.

Intellect, for Augustine, is light. Or rather, intellect is the place of light, for the light in which we see, and reason, and judge, and calculate, and predict, and explain – all those things which we here do in the university with such driven intensity – that light is in us, but not of us. We could not, Augustine thinks, do those things which are most ours as human unless there were that 'more' in us which is not ours: and that 'more' is the divine light, the light of 'eternal truth', he says. And intellect, for Augustine, gets its meaning as 'spirit' as that place on which our whole being is centred, a place which is, as it were, in a double relation of proximity. For it is the narrow point on which the immortality of truth converges with our mortality, where eternity intersects with our temporality, where the divine necessity meets with our contingency. Intellect, for Augustine, lives on a knife-edge, or rather it is the light by which we know and acknowledge the knife-edge on which our lives are precariously poised, perilously close both to death and to life, both to the nothingness from which we are created and to the eternal life for which we are created. To know that is to know oneself, it is to know how one's life is made and what it is for, it is to know all creation for what it most truly is. It is to know creation as Julian of Norwich saw it, as a hazelnut in the palm of her hand, a thing so small and precarious that she wondered how it could exist at all, until she saw that 'love made it' and alone held it secure in existence.

Julian saw this vision, and her seeing it is intellect, and her intellect is light; and what intellect sees is love, it sees that it is love alone which retrieves our existence from a condition so close to nothingness that there is nothing of ourselves which can separate us from it, nothing other than that divine love by which we are created. If we did not see love, then there would be nothing for it but a nihilistic despair: for an intellect, which sees everything else in so clear a light, if it does not see love, will see straight through everything, for the density of things is the love by which they are made; and in seeing nothing, because seeing through everything, that intellect is the most humanly destructive force of all. Intellect, so deprived, is a harlot, of whose power to subvert selfhood sexual harlotry is but a mere, and pale, inadequate, metaphor.

Which is why, St Bonaventure tells us, the light in which we see cannot itself be anything seen. What we see is light refracted off opaque objects in the densities of colour, and the loveliness of light is in the loveliness of its refractions. We can no more see God than we can see light itself, and so when we turn our minds from the solid opacities of creation towards the divine light in which we see them, we see nothing at all. Colour is light in its most material form; colour is light condensed and, as it were, congealed into opacity, denseness, colour is light become a thing to be seen. Creation is the visibility of the Godhead, for 'no one has seen God'; creation is, as it were, God's density, dense with the density of the love by which it is given, creation is the love of God congealed. We might say that God is love, pure love: and that is why we cannot see God, for the exposure of our minds to so searing a power would burn them to a cinder – as on Mount Sinai, God says to Moses 'no one may see my face and live' (Exodus 33.20). We cannot see that love in itself, but only in what is loved by it.

Creation is the colour of God, the unseeable light as visible, refracted, as it were, into the million pieces of a stained glass window; it is the deep silence of God existing as song, a song which exists, therefore, only so long as it is being sung. That we do not know the singer but only the song does not matter, for the singer has disappeared into his song, and to suppose we may love the singer but despise that song is a perversion of spirit, a 'strenuousness of thought' which, for sure, will keep us from our God.

And that song is us, and it is each other, and all creation as loved; and it is Jesus Christ, the most beloved of all creation, the song of the silent love of God. And he came among us. And then we killed him.

18

Dominus Illuminatio Mea

So reads the motto of the University of Oxford. But how does one preach to this university on that motto – or, as I suppose we should call it nowadays, its 'mission statement'? How, more generally, does one preach to any university? How is one supposed to do so, at any rate, in times when academics all too commonly perceive their universities' academic purposes in terms of a religious and moral neutrality, in terms of an exploratory openness, which *conflicts* with the intellectually closed, morally prescriptive purposes which, again, all too commonly, preaching is thought to serve. For which reason most universities allow no place for preaching within their official acts. Yet here at Oxford, as in my own university at Cambridge, a university preacher performs a public office, a duty the university as such discharges by delegation. Can its doing so be justified?

And as for me, though elected to a chair of Divinity in your sister university, preaching – understood in those terms of contrast – comes no more naturally to me in my academic *persona* than it does to an academic *persona* in any other discipline. I *teach* theology. I no more *preach* theology than a biologist preaches biology: indeed, working as we do in a discipline more vulnerable than most to criticism on that score, we theologians are perhaps more sensitive than most to the distinctions between teaching and preaching. And perhaps we are even excessively defensive. In any case, I suspect that I am rather less inclined to preach my subject professionally in my university than a certain well-known evolutionary biologist appears inclined to preach his subject in yours. At least I do not promote my subject in exclusion of his, as he promotes his in exclusion of mine.

And then, even were it clear that a university has a duty to be preached to, and even were it clear why its purposes imposed that obligation, you and I could well be asked what could justify a preaching on behalf of a *Christian* faith and tradition, in a *Christian* church, within a *Christian* service, to a university most of whose members do not, as university officers, have any loyalties to that

Church – and in any case, in their personal capacities may have loyalties or personal convictions which actually conflict with Christian faith. Ought I be *allowed* to do this?

I do not intend to answer these questions now. But if I do not answer them I ask them all the same, because they make me a little uneasy, and perhaps they make you uneasy too. So if I leave them unanswered, the questions still hover over our present act as a scruple about what we are doing here. Moreover, they arise not only on this particular university occasion, but also generally for our society as a whole, for our culture, of which this university, at least in respect of its diversity of beliefs, is a microcosm. And in either case, at the very least they demand some sort of answer to another, and more immediate, question which arose for me as I thought about how to speak to you today – when I considered, that is to say, not only what to preach *about*, but what preaching might *be* in these circumstances. I wondered about this, and I felt tempted to ask you if you knew what it is that you had invited me to do, if you knew what preaching *could possibly be* when delivered amidst such a confusion of unanswered questions addressed to us by our culture's pluralist convictions. So I do ask, because I want to know: what is it to preach in these circumstances in which multiple questions arise, to be compounded by answers as many times fudged?

I suppose at the very least, you preach for a moral purpose, to encourage a human value, a way of life, or a judgement about how to live. And if not necessarily *to* a community which shares that moral purpose with you – for you do not preach only to the converted – then at any rate preaching is done *on behalf of* a community on whose common moral purposes and traditions you draw. You do not exactly 'preach' when you speak out of a purely personal conviction, though you might hector, or barrack, or seek to persuade, or polemicize. Otherwise, the notion of a 'personal crusade' smacks of the oxymoronic, so that it is quite as hard in its own, different, way to know how to describe what your evolutionary biologist is up to in his anti-religious campaigning within the academy as it is to know what to make of preaching in that same context. You need a religious tradition to preach on behalf of, and certainly in my own Christian tradition stern warnings are found against preaching in your own name: Paul vehemently denied that he preached 'Paul', or that Apollo preached 'Apollo' or Peter 'Peter'. And Jesus himself told his followers that they were on no account to call themselves

'Rabbis', or 'teachers', for we have only one such, our Father in heaven, who teaches us all in common. So here, perhaps, our problem is acute.

For if you can say that you preach to a *moral* purpose, you can say that you teach at least to a *common* purpose; and in the same way, you teach from *out of* a shared tradition of learning; and you do so within and on behalf of a community bound together by its loyalties to those purposes and traditions. And this university is one such community. But what loyalties bind us if not a shared understanding of what we are as an *academic* community, of what it is to *teach*? And have we not come so to understand teaching that the sort of community from which you could *preach* is said to be without any rights of official influence, if not of informal presence, among us? For if as academics we teach any 'way of life', we say that we teach not any particular choice of how to live, but neutrally between them all: we teach 'life skills', we say, we teach skills of *choosing* with intellectual integrity, so that it is not to the choices themselves, but to the values of intellectual integrity in choosing, that we owe our responsibilities. But here I am, preaching not merely *as it happens* to some university people, but discharging a responsibility which this university continues officially to lay upon itself to commend to itself its own motto. And that motto declares that it is *the Lord* which is our light. And leaving, as I say to fudge, the question 'How can this be justified?' I ask the question: 'What, in such contradictory circumstances *is* this act of preaching?' How do you do it? As having what and whose authority as prescription can we say to one another, *Dominus illuminatio mea*?

You might suppose that this is not a new question, that it arises from an old and familiar anxiety of a dissenting sort. And you might think that I ask it out of a disenchantment with the establishment of a particular Christian Church, a disenchantment you might find unsurprising in an adherent of our history's oldest dissenting tradition, the Roman Catholic. For sure it was we dissenters who founded – or at least funded – my three former universities, at Birmingham, Bristol and in Dublin, and in each case, with the open intention of ruling out any possibility of an Anglican hegemony, ensured their radical secularization. Religious men as they were, Quakers and Catholics, those founders preferred to exclude in principle all possibility of official preaching than permit any privilege to the establishment form of it, because they saw an incompatibility between the official purposes of teaching and any official purpose of preaching. Dissensions among Christians have ever thus spawned secularizing children, if only, as Marx pointed out, thereby to encourage the growth and proliferation of religious faiths as privatized, displacing, as he put it, 'faith in authority' with 'the authority of faith'. And by now that conception of religious faith as being – in its very character *as* faith – essentially 'private' is just about as official an ideology of our secularized universities as any is. Well, you *might* think that my anxieties are of this dissenting, secularizing kind, but you would be wrong, they are not. I do not think that faith is inherently a private affair, even if universities have no business imposing any particular faith upon themselves. I do think that universities may legitimately oblige themselves to be preached to, and may do so consistently with their academic purposes. All the same, there remains this problem about what preaching can count as, for the voice of the preacher sounds a note discordant within the clamour of our teaching voices, just as your university's motto, declaring that it is *the Lord* who is our light, is not any longer, as it once was, a summons to a flag universally commanding the loyalties of its members.

So if we are to retrieve ourselves from hopeless muddle – I mean, if we here today, doing what we are doing are to make any sense of it – if we are to get anywhere, I think we need to start again from somewhere else than these trite distinctions between teaching and preaching. Perhaps the contrast between preaching and teaching is wrongly stated as that between the prescriptivity of the one and the value-neutrality of the other. For teaching like preaching has not only a common, but also a *moral* purpose. 'Heaven doth with us, as we with torches do, not light them for themselves' says the Duke to Angelo in Shakespeare's *Measure for Measure*. He goes on: 'for if our virtues did not go forth of us, 'twere all alike // as if we had them not'. And as with virtue so with knowledge. Thomas Aquinas, considering the relative merits of the contemplative and active lives, commends the mixed life above all, which combines the work of contemplation with that of teaching. For, he says, it is better to cast light upon others than merely to shine for oneself; therefore, the highest manner of life is that whose purpose is *contemplata aliis tradere*, to pass on to others the things contemplated: to be the bearer of light is necessarily to *cast* it. There is something frustrating not merely of a private ambition but of the very creative act itself in the sad plight of the unpublished Gerard Manley Hopkins, complaining: 'this to hoard unheard, heard unheeded, leaves me a lonely began'.

Because we are learners, we are teachers. It is in the nature of the light of learning that it should shine on others, so that it follows – if not a teacher then not a learner, but at best a sad and 'lonely began'. But what of that light itself, the *illuminatio* of the University's motto? How can we say that it is the Lord? Whose Lord? Our Christian creator Lord? Well, yes, I should say, but let me begin with a more ancient, non-Christian, authority, with Plato.

Plato detested the postmodern pluralists of his day, above all for their influence on the minds of the young, which, he thought, they infected with a sort of pedagogical relativism. He called them with heavy irony 'sophists', wise men, but in truth, he thought they were but '*merchants* of wisdom', though this was not merely because they demanded payment for their teaching. More fundamentally, he thought it possible for them to conceive of selling their teaching only because they had in any case reduced knowledge itself to a sort of commodity – the sort of thing you could *exchange* for some other commodity of equivalent value. The sophists, as Plato represents them, thought that knowledge 'got you places' – indeed, it *was* knowledge only if it got you places. The knowledge they purveyed served you well for a career in Athens if that's where you were, but would serve just as well for a career in Corinth or Alexandria if that's where you wanted to go, for the sort of knowledge which commanded a price on their market was that which guaranteed a successful career *anywhere at all*, regardless of the diversities of values, moral and intellectual, which characterized the cultures of these diverse polities. Therefore, the sophists taught principally forensic skills, the skills of public life, skills neutral as between competing claims to 'the good' – they taught, he said, a 'rhetoric', which could serve any end at all, any interest, any manner of life, anywhere at all, at least within the 'civilized' world. In short, the sophists taught what we call 'transferable skills'.

Therefore, Plato thought, the sophist's knowledge, useful 'everywhere', was a knowledge rooted in a 'nowhere', a deracinated, alienated, 'nowhere knowledge' of morally neutral intellectual 'skills', skills valued *because of* their 'transferability', their disponibility to any end regardless. Recognize the model? We call it 'postmodern', at any rate in a popular, non-technical sense, there being for neither the ancient nor the postmodern relativists any overarching, 'grand narratives', nothing 'given' with any finality, nothing having any value except in terms of what you can substitute for it, and it for. And, like Plato, I perceive this 'postmodern' mentality to be, in essence, but the market reconceived as intellect, for its model is the conversion of a *good*, a 'use-value', into an exchange-value. At any rate, so far as intellect goes, it is what will be paid for, then by the aristocratic youth of Athens, today by governments. And to be sure, what government today would pay for an annual output of half a million true but unprofitable Socrateses, when there are sophists available who will yield a measurable economic return on its investment?

We, in any case, no longer even dream of reconnecting, as Plato did, the idea of intellect with that of a 'common good', for we are as impressed with the moral pluralism of our day as the sophists were with the pluralism of theirs. Still, there remains something in Plato's vision which jogs the memory, and I do not mean that he reminds us of some lost times in our history when we too made that connection, for I doubt if we ever did. I mean rather that for Plato *all* learning was in the way of having your memory jogged and that all teaching was a form of memory-jogging. Plato meant that intellect was governed by a form of desire all of its own, an *eros*, a yearning and a longing for something beyond the immediately given, something which cannot be captured or ever finally possessed, for that 'beyond', that *chora* or 'space' of ultimate mystery to which it most truly belongs because it is where intellect has come from, its 'home'. And that 'home', from which we are in some way separated, is its good to which it seeks endlessly to return.

Therefore, Plato thought, all learning is an *anamnesis*, an unforgetting, a *reminding* of something it already in some way knows, but has lost sight of, and in his dialogue the *Meno*, he has Socrates demonstrate this by eliciting a proof of a geometric theorem from an innumerate slave-boy, by the device of asking only questions – though one has to say that, the questions being of a rather 'leading' sort, the demonstration is less than fully convincing. Be that as it may, there is something in what Plato says about teaching being a form of 'reminding' which we teachers all know when we have taught our students well, even when it is something in their experience seemingly quite new and surprising. It happened to us, if we were lucky in our teachers when we were students, to be struck by this or that paradox, which at once turned everything you thought you knew upside down and at the same time appeared so absolutely right, *just so*. And when we teach, do we not on such occasions elicit from our students a glint of *recognition* (which is just the Latin word for 'being reminded') which seems to say: 'How surprising, but *of course*, that is how it must be, it *fits*'- as if with something they had already known and have been caused to remember, something therefore 'as ancient as it is new', as Augustine said, *tam antiqua, tam nova*?

I do not think that this is entirely far-fetched. St Augustine certainly did not think so. When he finally discovered God it was, he said, in memory that he found him. In fact he thought that memory was the seat of *all* intellect, for intellect is but memory's desire, a desire to reconnect its broken lines of continuity with its own source. Intellect is moved to know by a kind of nostalgia for its own cause and origin. And that cause and origin is the divine light of truth which is at once in it, but not of it, at once the origin and goal of intellect's desire, 'ancient' as origin, 'new' as goal.

Therefore, if we are to say that for Augustine intellect is a sort of nostalgia, we will have to say that it is, paradoxically, a nostalgia not alone for an ancient origin, but also for an as yet unrealized future. For Augustine abandoned, as inconsistent with his Christian faith, Plato's teaching in the *Meno* and the *Phaedo*, that our souls had once known all truth in a pre-natal condition of separation from the body and had been caused to forget it all through the catastrophe of birth. For Augustine we are beings of eternal destiny inserted into contingency and time, and it is that very contingency and temporality of our worldly condition which 'reminds' us of an incomprehensible 'otherness', a strangeness of possibility, a strangeness which is at the same time familiar, like the strange familiarity of a home we return to after a long journey abroad. That familiar 'otherness' is also like a horizon; it surrounds all our knowledge, but can never be contained within it. For whenever we look *at* a horizon it is always contained within another beyond it. As Bonaventure centuries later was to put it: the light *in which* we see can never itself be the *object of* our seeing. This horizon, this light, may have a name, but if so, it is a name the meaning of which is incomprehensible to us, known because accounting for what we do know, but not itself an object of knowledge, just as we can see light in its refractions off opaque objects, though it is not in itself one of the things seen. Indeed, if we *could* see the light as an object, we would be unable to see anything *in it*. And so, Bonaventure says, this light is also a kind of darkness, a 'cloud of unknowing'. *Dominus illuminatio mea*.

But if this dark light is indeed named by the name 'Lord', it almost does not matter if the name is not admitted, or even if it is denied, so long as we are possessed by that 'nostalgia' which is the desire for it, that desire of intellect to know what must altogether transcend our knowing. And that desire comes back to our experience, in our university terms, as that most fundamental, but also that most familiar, of all our responsibilities, which is to intellect's unstoppable questioning, that openness to what lies unreachably beyond it.

And I do really think that this teaching and learning, governed by this desire to know, is all by itself, and without the need for anything else to make it so, a 'spirituality', one way into the reality and meaning of the Holy Spirit, our one common teacher. And if I might for a moment be a bit personal without, I hope, being merely pious, since the age of five – and therefore for fifty-five years – I have been at school, among learners and teachers, young and old of both kinds, among and from whom I have learned what it is to love learning. And what I have learned from them is what Augustine knew so well, and it is that to love learning is to be in love with love. For learning is a kind of loving, a desire whose object is an *infinite* truth and an *infinite* beauty. Jean Leclerq's *The Love of Learning and the Desire for God* is not perhaps quite my favourite book; but his is my favourite book title, except perhaps that I should want to say with greater emphasis that the love of learning *is* the desire for God. For sure, a teaching and a learning which lacks that 'infinity' to it, are nothing but forms of pedantry. It is not easy to know how to say these things today, the vocabularies ringing to contemporary ears but archaically, of those things which so reached into the hearts not only of Augustine, but also of Plato, and Aristotle, and Plotinus, and Hugh of St Victor, and Bonaventure and Thomas Aquinas and so many others since. They knew of intellect as a longing impossible to satisfy except in an infinitely beautiful truth. What I do know is that I have never known a student genuinely desiring to know who was able to be satisfied with less, though I have known a tragic few who seemed not to want to know at all; nor of a teacher who succeeded in doing more (though I have known a few who aspired to less) than to evince a trace of memory, an instinct and a passion already there in them, to love God with their minds also.

We teachers may aspire to nothing less, and can hope to achieve no more, than this 'reminding' that our desire has but an infinite horizon, a horizon whose infinity discloses in us an infinite capacity for it. This unknowable horizon, this unseeable light, which surrounds and governs our learning, is no predetermined boundary at which knowledge must stop, some point of finality which could extinguish the desire to know. It is an enticement, a seduction, a sort of *ecstasis* of mind, which draws the mind out of itself into the infinity of space which is its own natural object, its 'home' – in that sense, the place it *already* knows. In the meantime, therefore, the human mind has no place of rest, but only a place of restlessness, of one single unsatisfiable passion: the desire to know. Such a place is what we continue to call a 'university'.

And yet, when we look at the state of our universities today, do we not see them to be under enormous pressures to bother with only such questions as have answers useful to our paymasters? That would be less worrying if it were not also the case that there are pressures from *within* our own company, intellectual pressures of a more theoretically positivist sort, which would persuade us that only such are legitimate questions which we know in advance we have the means in principle to answer – sensible questions whose route to an answer is governed by agreed methodologies. Make no mistake. Most of what we do, very properly, has this character. We train our students of history to ask the sorts of questions to which historical evidence can yield answers; physicists to ask questions about the universe which a physicist can answer; philosophers to ask philosophical questions and not historical or scientific. Finding the right routes from question through evidence to answer is what we do, most of the time. But there is danger within all this, the danger that we will reverse the traffic between question and answer so as to permit only such questions to be asked as we already possess predetermined methodologies for answering, cutting the agenda of questions down to the shape and size of our given routines for answering them.

And it is just here that we need to be reminded: *Dominus illumin-atio mea*. For there is an arrogance, peculiar to intellectuals, in supposing that that alone deserves to be called *real* which is predetermined in our given methods of enquiry, an arrogance and a provinciality of mind which is also a servile flattery of the reductivist, utilitarian and philistine spirit of our age; for, like every other age, as Marx pointed out, our age permits to be asked of itself only such questions as it can answer. Each age, therefore, will have a reason for refusing theological questions, for the proper territory of the theological is precisely that of the unknowable and the unsayable, of the question which is unanswerable, of which territory it is its proper role to remind us. If the theologians will not defend this territory – worse, if they are denied the right to do so – then who can be counted upon to do so? But even if theology as such were denied this right, to entertain the possibility that in each of our disciplines we are drawn to know by a desire whose goal is in principle unknowable in any of them, is a kind of humility, a sort of awe, a 'fear' which is the beginning of wisdom. *Dominus illuminatio mea.* But the psalm goes on in the Vulgate: *quem timebo?* Of what indeed should we be in awe, but of that light itself and the infinite challenge which it throws down before us? And if in awe of that light and of the responsibilities it places on us to know, what questions, however hard, however disturbing, need we fear to entertain? Therefore, even if, in our postmodern times, we cannot any longer count on all agreeing that it is our creator Lord and saviour who is our light, can we not at least agree that it is that light, experienced if only anonymously as that insatiable desire to know, which is the Lord, ruling and governing our work here, and learn to fear our responsibilities to it?

It is here, at this point, that the work of teaching and the work of preaching coincide in a common purpose and foundation. It is of this that universities can require themselves to be from time to time reminded, namely that they themselves are places of memory, with a purpose of reminding which serves an *infinite* good, a good surpassing all utility because it breaks through the bounds of any calculation which could possibly measure it. All religion teaches that in order *even* to be human, we must have the humility to be *more than* human, to acknowledge in humility the paradox that we can humanly know our end to transcend our human powers to an unknowable degree, that we are by finite nature inserted into an infinite demand made upon us. It is the same in the order of knowledge. What we do or can know, we know only because of a light which is unknowable, and so the desire to know is an infinite passion. And whether or not you wish so to name it, that unknowable light is, as Thomas Aquinas says, what the name 'God' refers to, and the desire for it truly an 'intellectual love of God'. Therefore, in truth, for this university as for any other, *Dominus illuminatio mea*. Of that, at least, we have a duty to remind ourselves.

Index of Names and Subjects